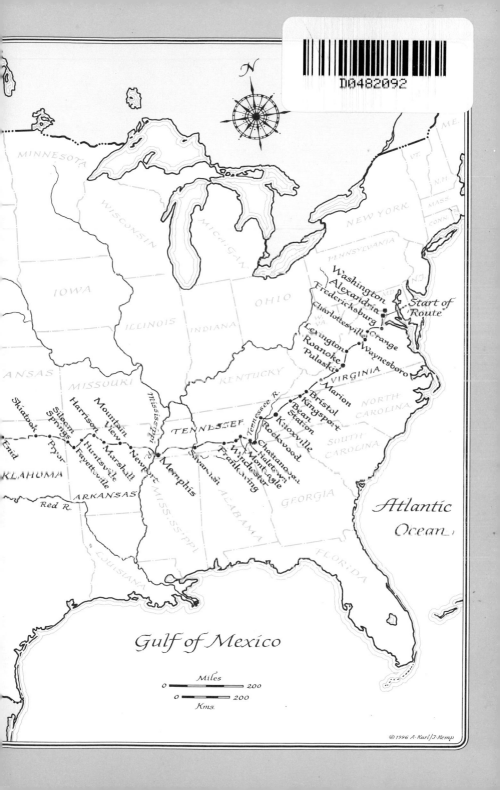

N

MINNESOTA

WISCONSIN

MICHIGAN

IOWA

OHIO

NEW YORK

VT.

N.H.

MASS.

CONN.

PENNSYLVANIA

ILLINOIS

INDIANA

Washington
Alexandria
Fredericksburg
Charlottesville Orange
Lexington
Roanoke Waynesboro
Pulaski
VIRGINIA

Start of
Route

ANSAS

MISSOURI

KENTUCKY

Mississippi R.

TENNESSEE

Marion
Bristol
Kingsport
Bean
Station
Knoxville

NORTH
CAROLINA

Tennessee R.

Skiatook
Siloam
Springs
Harrison
Mountain
View
Marshall
Huntsville
Fayetteville
Newport

Rockwood
Rockwood
Chattanooga
Haletown
Mont Agle
Winchester
Franklin

SOUTH
CAROLINA

Enid
Pryor

Memphis

OKLAHOMA

ARKANSAS

Swan si

ALABAMA

GEORGIA

Red R.

LOUISIANA

MISSISSIPPI

FLORIDA

Atlantic
Ocean

Gulf of Mexico

Miles
0 ——————— 200

0 ——————— 200
Kms.

© 1996 A·Karl/J·Kemp

OVER THE HILLS

OVER THE HILLS

A MIDLIFE ESCAPE ACROSS AMERICA BY BICYCLE

David Lamb

TIMES BOOKS

RANDOM HOUSE

All rights reserved under International and Pan-American
Copyright Conventions. Published in the United States by
Times Books, a division of Random House, Inc., New
York, and simultaneously in Canada by Random House of
Canada Limited, Toronto.

Library of Congress Cataloging-in-Publication
data is available.
ISBN 0-8129-2579-3

Printed in the United States of America on acid-free paper
2 3 4 5 6 7 8 9
First Edition
Book design by Deborah Kerner

For Peg Northrop

Long live the bicycle!
It is a friend to man, like the horse.
—HENRY MILLER

Get a bicycle.
You will not regret it if you live.
—MARK TWAIN

It does not fit that every man should travel;
it makes a wise man better, and a fool worse.
—OWEN FELTHAM

Contents

OVER THE HILLS

Introduction

I SLIPPED PAST FIFTY AND INTO MIDDLE AGE WITHOUT A whimper, my life in good working order. I liked my job, loved my wife, had enough money for a summer vacation. I was tiresomely reliable and responsible. True, I had grown weary of putting out the trash Tuesday nights and worrying whether my IRA was growing fast enough, but as I approached the eve of my fifty-fifth birthday, my assessment was that I wasn't suffering any midlife crisis at all. I felt normal to a fault. But normalcy is a heavy burden to carry when you're a rogue at heart, and for some time I had been plotting to break the bonds of convention. I didn't want to feel ordinary anymore. The plan that evolved was simple and was in a way, I suppose, an echo from adolescence: I would get on my bicycle and disappear on the back roads of America, following whatever ribbon of highway I found, from my home in Virginia to California.

Although my bicycling during the past forty years had been limited to an occasional Sunday ride of no more than a few miles, the notion of heading out alone was not entirely out of character for me. Contentment makes me restless, and restlessness is both a curse and a blessing that I have always tried to act on. It has summoned me far, carrying me by Greyhound and trailer truck and RV to every corner of the land, and at times made me feel as though I could be quite fulfilled

3

wandering aimlessly forever. I wanted assurances that I could still kick those muses into gear. The thought of ever becoming a nine-to-fiver whose idea of exhilaration was a weekend in Ocean City frightened me.

There was another motivation, too. As a journalist, I had built a career living off the adventures—and often misfortunes—of others. I had spent a dozen years in Australia, Asia, Africa and the Middle East, traipsed through battlefields from Vietnam to Rwanda, crisscrossed America a hundred times. But I was the interloper, the silent observer who dared not be the protagonist. It had, in fact, been years since I had taken on a challenge requiring discipline and endurance that had nothing to do with fulfilling professional obligations.

My intent in biking from the Potomac to the Pacific was to do what I most enjoy: dawdle and hang out. I have seldom encountered a saloon or a café I didn't like, and I would be bound by no schedules, no timetables. I would stick to the back roads, stay in motels whenever possible instead of camping and, I promised my wife, call home every night. Among the items I packed in my saddlebags were a cellular phone, a four-pound computer and fourteen maps.

In the weeks before my departure, well-meaning friends buried me with advice. They sent books on establishing a regimen of exercise that appeared designed for a soldier going to war. There were others on high-energy diets that featured god-awful food and completely ignored the fact that I've steered clear of most carbohydrates ever since restaurants started calling spaghetti pasta. And the books on bicycling were full of such arcane stuff about gear ratios and training techniques that computers seemed simple in comparison. The pile of advice on my desk grew higher and I wondered if we hadn't become so preoccupied with health and looking good that we expended all our energy preparing instead of doing. Had we all forgotten the can-do American spirit when we hitched up our pants and said, "Let's just do it"?

Even my doctor was a skeptic. "Look at this," he said, tapping the printout of a lab test. "Your cholesterol is 270. That's dangerously high. I'm going to put you on medication." I protested. Fifteen years earlier my level was 285 and I was told I was in excellent health. My cholesterol goes *down* and *now* I'm at risk? "The standard has changed," he said. Then, looking at the pack of cigarettes in my shirt pocket, he added: "You've got to quit those things if you want to make it over the mountains. And I'd refrain from alcohol if I were you." I nodded but wasn't sure I wanted to use the journey to remake myself into a man of the nineties.

For a good many months the idea of biking across America at an age when I should have known better flitted about as little more than a lark. It was on the list of things that would be fun to do when I retired or hit the lottery, like going to a major league baseball fantasy camp or circling the globe on the *QE2*, and it wasn't until friends kept doubting me— "You have as much chance making it to California as you do getting to the moon," one said—that the journey took on a life of its own and became something I was determined to do. I spent Saturdays at my local library, reading books on bicycling history, and discovered true adventurers who had crossed a largely roadless America by bicycle a century ago, as well as advocates for women's rights like Susan B. Anthony, who said in 1896 that the bicycle had done more to emancipate women than anything in the world. "I stand and rejoice every time I see a woman ride on a wheel," she said. "It gives women a feeling of freedom and self-reliance." I learned that bicyclists, not motorists, led the campaign to improve the nation's abominable roads at the turn of the century and that the sociological impact of the bicycle on society was, relatively speaking, nearly as significant as that of the automobile.

Although I grew up in a time when an adult riding a bike was considered a nerd, times have clearly changed. There are 120 million bicycles today in the United States, which is more per capita than there are in India or China, and biking has become the third most popular recreational sport in the country, after exercise walking and swimming. Still, by viewing the bicycle as an adult toy, we misunderstand its importance and usefulness: Bicycles remain the most efficient means of self-propulsion ever invented and the prime source of transportation for most of the world's population.

The bicycle I chose to carry me to California was a Trek 520, forest green, American-made, with twenty-one gears and a sleek, handsome appearance, not at all like the fat-tired, aluminum-coated Schwinn I had ridden as a teenager and relegated to a basement closet when I turned old enough to drive.

The Friday before Labor Day broke clear and crisp along the Potomac. A hint of autumn was about. It was a morning when the thought of going to work was the least appealing of life's options. I lingered over the newspaper and drank an extra cup of coffee. Then, instead of walking up King Street to catch the Metro train into Washington, D.C., I wrestled my bicycle off the ceiling hook in our sunroom closet and wheeled it into the backyard. I loaded up four saddlebags and strapped them over the front and rear axles.

My wife, Sandy, eyed me with a combination of disbelief and amusement. "Are you sure you've got enough underwear?" she asked. I said two pairs of padded briefs were ample. I pushed the bicycle into the alleyway, struggling to keep it upright because of the unexpected weight of the fat saddle-bags. I mounted, turned right out of the alley and started pedaling for Los Angeles, three thousand miles away.

At age fifty-four, having trained hardly at all, beset by all the uncertainties of middle age, knowing little about bicycles except how to change a flat tire, I was heading out on the most foolhardy adventure of my life. The America I saw in my mind's eye was flat as an ironing board, with gentle winds that blew at my back. I hesitated to even think about the Smokies and Rockies and the other mountain chains that would block my passage.

Sandy stood in the alley as I pedaled out of our backyard. I did not dare wave good-bye for fear I would tip over if I released either hand from the handlebar. Rush-hour traffic was in full force. I tried to keep as far to the right as possible and at the first red light, I pulled to the curb, my front wheel jutting into the pedestrian walkway for a fast getaway. My position briefly blocked the path of a car turning right. The driver rolled down his window and yelled, "Asshole!"

ONE

FROM THE POTOMAC
TO THE TENNESSEE MOUNTAINS

*When you get to
the fork in the road,
take it.*
—YOGI BERRA

1

MY HOME IN ALEXANDRIA, VIRGINIA, JUST ACROSS THE PO-
tomac from Washington, is a two-story brick row house that,
until gentrification took hold in the community during the
1970s, was part of a city slum. It sits seven blocks from one of
the nation's great networks of bicycle trails—an intercon-
necting, off-road linkage that stretches hundreds of miles,
along the reclaimed track bed of the Washington and Old
Dominion Railroad and the resurfaced mule towpath of the
Chesapeake and Ohio Canal, past monuments honoring
Washington, Jefferson and Lincoln, through parks and suburbs, over hills and into the farmland of Virginia, West Virginia, Maryland and Pennsylvania. The pathways are mostly
paved, sheltered by trees from the headwinds and the exclu-
sive domain of bikers, joggers, walkers, horseback riders and
Rollerbladers. I have always thought of them as proof that
civilization has not abandoned our cities entirely.

I wanted to get out of the heavy traffic, and I turned down Duke Street to the bike path that runs along the Potomac to George Washington's home at Mount Vernon, ten miles south. It was 9:15 A.M. No one else was playing hookey that morning, and I labored along an empty trail, the thirty pounds of weight in my saddlebags—or "panniers," as cyclists like to call them—making each pedal stroke feel as though I were biking through wet cement. The digital odometer clipped to my handlebar said I was doing eleven miles an hour. California seemed an unspeakable distance away, in miles and spirit, and I heard a voice whisper, "Okay. The joke's over. Go on home now and get dressed for work."

The only cyclist I passed en route to Mount Vernon was lying supine on the path at the foot of a small hill. My first thought was that he was the victim of a bikejacking—an increasingly common crime in the Washington area—but then I saw a park policeman hunkered over him, tending to his injuries. I heard the officer radio for an ambulance and the biker say, "I know it wasn't here yesterday. I wasn't expecting it." The officer nodded. A construction hose stretched across the bike lane nearby. I dismounted and walked my bike around it and the downed cyclist. A few feet into the hill, having forgotten to shift into a lower gear, I slipped my feet back into the toe clips, rose up in the saddle to get some momentum and went nowhere. The bike wavered, then in slow motion tumbled onto its side, with me bolted to the saddle. I felt like a boob but was relieved that I hadn't caught the attention of the policeman or any passing bikers. Here I was looking for all the world like a serious cross-country tourer, dressed in the latest biking gear from the Performance catalog, riding an expensive bike designed for business, and I couldn't make it five miles from home without crashing. My knee was bloodied and my pride bruised. The joking words spoken by a friend a few days earlier floated back: "Lamb, this trip of yours sounds like it involves more style than substance." I feared he might be right and knew I was getting into something for which I was shamefully ill prepared.

Ahead, Mount Vernon was starting to fill up. Tour buses and out-of-state cars crowded the parking lot and a brigade of visitors already were prowling the estate, which Washington ran with the help of three hundred slaves and hired hands. I stopped for coffee and a smoke. With my bulging saddlebags and battered knee, the bike balanced on its kickstand a few feet away, it should have been apparent to anyone that something interesting was under way here. A middle-aged man approached wearing an Oakland Raiders sweatshirt. I hoped he would ask where I was headed, so I could casually respond "California," but after pausing for a moment, apparently not having even noticed my bike, he said, "Say, bub, you tell me where the toilets are?" I suppose I could have been sitting in a Conestoga wagon and all he would have wanted to know was where he could take a leak.

Mount Vernon, a comfortable hour's ride from home, had been my destination in several previous weekend jaunts. I had never biked farther because the bike path ends there and venturing onto heavily traveled Route 1 on a bicycle seemed foolish. So I'd eat one of Mount Vernon's overcooked hamburgers, which tasted like a mouthful of newsprint, and take a leisurely ride home, where I'd shower and open a beer. It made for a nice afternoon. As I sat there, finishing my coffee, the thought of simply turning around and biking back to

Sandy and familiar surroundings was a pleasing one. I didn't even know where I would end the day's travels, much less where I would spend the night, and as much as I liked to think of myself as an adventurer, too much uncertainty made me uneasy.

Route 1 is the granddaddy of all U.S. highways, reaching 2,425 miles from Fort Kent, Maine, to Key West, Florida. First known as the Indian Trial, then the Potomac Path, the King's Highway and the Old Telegraph Line Road, it served the original thirteen colonies as a wagon trail fifty years before George Washington was born. As recently as 1951 it carried more passengers and freight than any road in the world. But Interstate 95 stole its travelers and its significance, relegating Route 1 to a short-haul road, an unsightly collection of fast-food chains and mom-and-pop businesses too small to set up shop in the malls. In an era when interstates have killed whole towns, as well as grand old roads like Route 66, it is the highway of survivors.

By more than coincidence, Route 1 follows the "fall line"—the ancient shore of the continent—from New Jersey to Georgia. This is where the rivers of the Eastern seaboard flowed out of the hills onto the coastal plain, marking the westernmost point that shippers could navigate inland. From the fall line, goods had to be transferred from boat to wagons for inland delivery and it is along this invisible boundary that the colonial settlements of Trenton, Philadelphia, Baltimore, Richmond, Raleigh, Columbia and Augusta sprang up at the banks of rivers. The trail that was forged through the wilderness to link this avenue of commerce eventually became Route 1. I watched the vehicles speed by on it, all four lanes clogged bumper to bumper. When the light turned green, I took a breath and headed for the far curbside lane as fast as I could pedal, slipping into a gap between two eighteen-wheelers and moving south with the traffic.

Cars swept by, just inches away, and passing trailer trucks sucked me into the whoosh of their vacuums. I dared not look right or left for fear I would stray from the white shoulder line I hugged. I was a moving target, as vulnerable as I had once been in Beirut when snipers tried to pick you off as you dashed across the "green line" that divided the city. A horn blared and the car roared by, its driver greeting me with an extended middle finger. "What's your problem, buddy?" I shouted, but my words were drowned in the rumble of traffic. The miles went slowly and I watched my odometer chronicling the widening distance from home: twenty-five miles . . . thirty . . . thirty-five . . .

In Fredericksburg, where sprawling development along the Rappahannock River has eaten up some of the nation's most important Civil War battlefields, I turned off Route 1 and on a side street found a shabby motel whose marquee said, "Air Cond. & TV." My legs were wobbly, my jersey wet with sweat. I knew I was going no farther. The owner was an Indian dressed in a red sari—Indians, I would discover, are taking over the small independent motels throughout the United States, just as the Chinese did the laundries a century ago—and she asked me if I wanted to see the room before paying.

"Why would I want to see the room?" I asked.

"What if it's not clean?" she said. "We don't give refunds after you pay."

I said I'd take my chances. She smiled and shrugged. I gave her twenty-eight dollars and pushed my bike across the parking lot and lugged it over the threshold of Unit 11. The room was decorated in the style of depression-era modern. Formica covered the furniture and the brown drapes were held closed by clothespins. The wastepaper basket was an empty container that, the label said, once held sixty pounds of Georgia-Pacific Joint Compound. The unflushed toilet bore reminders of the last occupant. But everything considered, after my knocking off fifty-two miles and surviving Route 1 and feeling none the worse for wear, the place was just fine. Best of all, across the street was an establishment called the Houston Steak House and Saloon and I felt like a quiet celebration.

Alone at the bar, I watched thirty or forty couples on the dance floor learning the "snakebite." Their teacher, a woman in a cowgirl's outfit who reminded me of Dale Evans, was saying, ". . . six, seven, eight, heels together, rock . . . one, two, three . . ." The scene belonged more to Montana than Virginia, and as the weekend cowboys half-stepped around the dance floor in their Stetsons, jeans and boots, I knew that we tenderfoots shared something in common: In the most innocent of ways, we had, however briefly, taken on new identities in the recesses of our imagination—they the wrangler whooping it up in the saloon of an old cow town, me the passing stranger, westbound, not always knowing why he moves but understanding that movement is a means of expression for those of us who feel at home on the open road.

2

FREDERICKSBURG DIVIDES THE TWO VIRGINIAS. NORTH OF town people identify themselves as *northern* Virginians or even Washingtonians. They don't speak with a drawl and are likely to have come from someplace else. But from Fredericksburg south, there are only Virginians. Not *southern* Virginians. Just *Virginians*. They've been around for generations, and on the playgrounds, their children still split into teams named Yanks and Rebels. Every time I venture onto their turf I have the feeling the nation's most recent war wasn't in Kuwait or Vietnam; it was in Virginia, where the Confederacy still stirs passions that mystify Northerners like myself. Da Nang is the past, Manassas the present; if only Pickett had managed to break the Northern lines at Gettysburg, if only Lee had triumphed at Antietam to carry the war above the Potomac . . .

Perhaps, though, it is a good thing Virginians cling to their history, because urban encroachment is swallowing up the South's battlefields from the Civil War—or the War of Northern Aggression, as Virginians call it—faster than they can be saved. I went looking for the tangled forests in Fredericksburg where two great armies met in hand-to-hand combat in 1862 and found only housing developments. New homes have claimed the last of three battlefields in Winchester, a town that changed hands so many times during the war—seventy-two by one count—that merchants kept two cash drawers, one for Confederate money, the other for Federal dollars. The Hazen monument, one of the Civil War's oldest memorials, now stands in the shadow of a cement factory at the Stones River battlefield in Tennessee. A large chunk of the Manassas battlefield was spared from development as a shopping mall only after public protests prodded a reluctant Congress into buying the disputed 542 acres for $120 million in 1989. The bloodied fields around the northern Virginia town of Haymarket were nearly turned into a Disney theme park in 1994 and not far off, in Brandy Station, site of the Civil War's largest cavalry battle, a Formula One racetrack is going up.

I turned off Route 1 and followed Route 3, then 20, through the rolling farmland where Grant and Lee fought the Wilderness campaign. For now the battlefield is pristine and quiet, out of reach of the expanding cities. But what makes the preservationists' task so daunting is that by 1860 the nation's transportation system was in place, and it was along those roads, railroads and waterways that the major Civil War battles were fought. Today's transportation pattern follows that of the nineteenth century, and the dirt roads of yesterday have become our four-lane thoroughfares linking rapidly growing urban areas. Unlike battlefields from the Indian wars (the most popular of which were fought in the still spacious West) and the Revolutionary War (which was characterized by small clashes in some now out-of-the-way places), the Civil War was fought in a wide path along what has emerged as the interstate system. These southern interstates—I-95 connecting Virginia, the Carolinas and Georgia; I-81 through Virginia's Shenandoah Valley; I-65, -24 and -75 from Louisville down through Tennessee to Atlanta—all have spawned massive growth, sprawling suburbs and soaring real estate prices. Suddenly it is no longer economically feasible to save farmland, much less historic sites that are not on the tax rolls.

The road I traveled was known as the Orange Turnpike during the Civil War and it was here that Stonewall Jackson led his troops on a risky twelve-mile march around Union lines, was wounded, and died after the amputation of an arm. The four lanes became two, traffic thinned. The road climbed and fell and I felt pleasantly alone, unhurried and unharried. It was Saturday. Fredericksburg was behind me. The occasional car that sped by acknowledged my presence by pulling toward the center line. Dense foliage closed in along the stone walls that paralleled the way and it was not difficult to hear the crackle of gunfire and imagine uniformed ghosts dashing among the trees. In a car, windows rolled up, radio on, I was isolated from the world around me. On a bicycle, I was part of it. I moved with it as much as I did through it.

My right knee sounded as though it needed lubricating at every stroke but I had struck a comfortable pace, thirteen or fourteen miles an hour on the flats; the songlike hum of my tires over pavement had a reassuring ring. I clicked off my odometer so I would be less conscious of the miles traveled and those that remained; the digital display now reported the temperature instead of the day's mileage. I passed through Chancellorsville, Rhoadesville, Unionville. There wasn't much in any of them, not even a coffee shop. I'd have traded my three boxes of raisins for a café where I could sit at the counter and read the morning paper over a cup of coffee and a cigarette. At home I keep coffee dripping through my system at a steady clip, so now I felt a knocking in the back of my head that I attributed to caffeine withdrawal. My focus blurred. I pulled off the road at a Y junction where several cars were parked and took a drink from one of my three water bottles. The water, warmed by the midday sun, tasted of plastic. Each of the containers attached to the frame of my bike weighed a pound and a half when full, and since, according to the laws of physics, every static pound is the equivalent of two rotating pounds, I decided to lighten my load. I emptied two of the bottles.

A sixteen-year-old girl named Becky and her younger brother, Michael, had set up shop at the junction and were doing a brisk business selling secondhand tires. They were terrific salesmen, examining the treads and worn spots on the tires of cars that stopped and making observations like "Don't imagine you've got more than a couple of hundred miles left on what you've got on." During a lull in negotiations, they wandered over to where I sat on a clump of grass. Becky wore cutoff jeans and a tight white blouse that gave a prominence to her chest. Michael was blond and lanky and looked as though he belonged in a field of golden hay. "That's some bike," he said, "but those tires look pretty bald to me." I said they were new and came treadless to reduce rolling resistance. Michael seemed disappointed. Becky tucked in her blouse and thrust back her shoulders and I thought she might be flirting.

I asked her if I'd find a motel in Orange, the next town, and she said, "Nah, Orange's a nothing town. I went to school there. There's nothing around here. You take Norfolk, Richmond, Roanoke, those are *cities*. But around here, you're lucky to find a place to go bowling. I'm gone soon as I'm old enough. My mama says I can do it as long as my man is loving. My fiancé, he's all of that. He's out in Oklahoma now and I already been there once to visit him. The day I turn eighteen, the very day, I'm gone for Oklahoma and we're getting married. The only problem is, he's got a big car that's a real gas guzzler and he says that's going to be mine and he's keeping the pickup."

I asked Becky what she liked about Oklahoma, and she said: "It ain't here."

A few minutes later I pedaled off, the long empty road ahead disappearing over the crest of a hill. I heard Becky call out, "Y'all have a safe journey." I left her with her tires and her dreams, not yet old enough to know how easy it is to move on nor wise enough to understand that sometimes the best part of moving on is coming home again.

3

BECKY WAS WRONG ABOUT THERE BEING NO PLACE TO STAY in Orange. A large motel stood just outside of town. Her oversight provided me with Road Lesson Number 1: What people tell bicyclists about road conditions and what lies ahead is usually wrong. If they say the road is smooth and downhill all the way to the next town, it's probably rough and a damn tough climb. If they say there's a motel ten miles away, it's probably twenty miles and it may have been turned into apartments a decade ago. The problem is that motorists perceive their surroundings in an entirely different manner than cyclists. Or more to the point, they don't perceive them at all. At a steady sixty miles an hour all the world looks the same, and who pays attention to whether the road goes up or down? At sixty, ten miles is ten minutes away. On a bicycle, it could be thirty minutes, or an hour or even two depending on the headwinds, the weather, the pavement. I grew cautious asking about the best routes or what was around the bend because strangers, ever eager to be helpful and to appear knowledgeable, would rather give you the wrong answer than no answer at all. In the end the only people whose advice I came to trust were long-distance truck drivers, highway patrolmen and, from Oklahoma westward, oil drillers.

"Yeah, I got a bunch of empty rooms," the man at the motel in Orange said. "They're *all* empty, but I can't rent you one. The flood in June put me out of business, ruined every room. Insurance is paying for lost revenue, so I'm not getting killed, but I can't rent anything until the renovation is finished. That's the deal with the insurance people. About ten miles down the road, in Charlottesville, you'll find plenty of places to stay."

Actually, Charlottesville was twenty-four miles away and here in the hill country that would take me a couple of hours and put me in after dark. "I'd be a goner riding this road at night," I said. The man looked at me, then at my bicycle. He was wavering. "How far'd you say you're goin'?" he asked.

"I'm trying to make it to California."

"Come on. I'll find you a bed."

He led me to a corner room in the empty, one-story motel. He brought in a phone and plugged it into the jack. He

turned on the electricity and water in my wing. He said not
to worry about bringing my bike into the room; he was tear-
ing out the carpet next week anyway.

"Just drop the key in the mailbox when you leave tomorrow," he said. Then he added, "The insurance people said I
couldn't rent any rooms, but they didn't say anything about
giving one away. There's no charge."

Road Lesson Number 2: Traveling by bicycle returns you
to an era when Americans had time to be gracious to a man
passing through and weren't afraid of each other. On my bike
I posed no threat. I could strike up a conversation with anyone, ask strangers for assistance, offer help to a woman alone
sitting in her stalled car on an empty stretch of highway. No
one questioned my intent or greeted me with eyes that
looked away. Four months earlier I had been in Rwanda for
the *Los Angeles Times,* writing about a massacre of unfath-
omable proportions, and had found it eerie that people did
not look one another in the eye. To make contact was perhaps to meet your executioner. So people kept their distance,
staying to themselves in small ethnic groups, and in the
process Rwanda ceased to exist as a civilized society. The
Rwandans shared a common language and a common border
but not the trust, civility and aspirations that bind a people as
a nation. They could travel no road without being fearful.

In that sense I felt fortunate here on Route 231. Though
friends had suggested I carry all manner of weapons on my
journey, nothing around me smelled of danger, and my only
protection was a small spray canister of gas to repel dogs. My
concerns consisted of little more than avoiding potholes and
finding a bed at day's end. It was the simplest, most uncom-

plicated of existences. Any Rwandan would have changed places with me in a heartbeat. When I left that cursed little country, no longer having to sleep on the hard ground under a tent or hold handkerchiefs to my nose to block out the stench of corpses, I promised myself I'd be more selective in what I found to complain about. Africa puts life back in perspective better than any other place I know, and at home, if the road seemed too long or lonely and a dark mood engulfed me, to regain my equilibrium I had only to say, "Hell, this isn't so bad. I could be in Rwanda."

I washed my padded briefs and socks in the sink, a daily chore I disliked but a necessary one to prevent fungus and rash. I wrung them out and hung them over a bush outside the door. I showered and changed into my chinos, cotton shirt and loafers. It was 7 P.M. What in the world was I going to do with the rest of the night? The nearest restaurant, a Dairy Queen, was a mile away, the closest bar a mile beyond that. The TV didn't work. I called Sandy. She wasn't home. My bike didn't need oiling. *Hell, this isn't so bad. I could be in . . .* I flopped on the bed and, for the first time in my life, picked up a Bible the Gideon Society had placed in the room. Ecclesiastes, chapter 3: "To every thing there is a season, and a time to every purpose under the heaven. . . ."

A few nights before leaving home, I made a list of what I needed to pack in my saddlebags and piled the items on a chair. It was the ultimate test of reducing life's necessities to the bare minimum. I called an acquaintance in California who had done a lot of bike touring and asked if she had any suggestions. "Sure do," she said. "Go through the stuff you're planning to pack and leave half of it at home. If you have to think twice about whether you need something, you don't.

Every pound you pack is another pound you're going to have to push over the mountains. Travel light." Reluctantly I returned the pint of Seagram's V.O. to my bar. I removed a hardback copy of Cormac McCarthy's *The Crossing,* two of five notebooks, the nail clippers, three rolls of film, an extra pair of chinos, the three-pound tent, the yellow rain gear (on the premise that if it rained I was going to get wet anyway) and, ludicrously enough, a pack of gum. What remained registered thirty-one pounds on my bathroom scale.

Figuring out how to pack the stuff wasn't at all like filling a suitcase. I rolled my clothes, instead of folding them, and placed them inside waterproof Ziploc bags. I put my four spare inner tubes into resealable plastic bags filled with talcum powder, which helps prevent tubes from getting "pinched" by the wheel's rim—a surefire way to develop a slow leak through two tiny punctures that resemble a snakebite. Then I tucked the contents of each saddlebag into plastic garbage bags in case I encountered a downpour. Most important, to facilitate steering and prevent the bike from tipping to one side or the other, the weight needed to be evenly divided among the four saddlebags. And the front saddlebags had to ride low and carry about 60 percent of the weight to establish the correct center of gravity and compensate for the fact that the rear half of an unloaded bike is heavier than the front half. Years ago I had worked for a trucking company, packing thirty-foot-long trailers with household goods, and I took pride in my ability to build a snug, tight load and fill each nook and cranny with precisely the right-sized carton or piece of furniture. Finding the proper home for each item that I slipped into my saddlebags was no less challenging or fun.

The handful of tools and the little kit to patch flats went in a pouch under the saddle, the camera, traveler's checks, note-books and Nicorette gum to cut down on my smoking into a bag attached to my handlebar, onto which was also clipped a compass and a small battery-powered headlight. The front saddlebags became the home for my computer, cellular phone, all the maps except the one needed to get me out of Virginia, toiletries in a Ziploc bag and a rolled-up windbreaker. In the left rear pannier I put an extra change of bike clothes—shorts, padded briefs, jersey and socks—and into the right one the set of street clothes that would enable me to enter a saloon or café at night without having to wear my identity as a bicyclist like a badge. I fastened a sleeping bag and an extra tire over the rear rack and a hand air pump alongside the down tube of the frame. By the time I finished, I had almost convinced myself that I knew what I was doing. But undeniably the bike had looked snazzy standing there in the sunroom of my home, loaded up and ready to run across an entire continent.

I dozed off in the shuttered motel reading the Bible and when I awoke it was nine o'clock. My sore knees had grown stiff. Damn, I thought, it'd be nice to have someone around to talk to. Reluctant to ride in the dark, I set off with a limp to the Dairy Queen. The place was full of teenagers, idling away another quiet night in another quiet town, and in twenty minutes I was in and out, my spirits restored by a health-conscious dinner: double burger, onion rings, Dr Pepper and a chocolate milk shake. On the way back to the motel, a car loaded with half a dozen kids slowed and some-one yelled, "Hey, mister, you wanna try riding?" I was about to shout back "Wise ass!" but realized I was putting a city in-terpretation on a country invitation: They were offering exactly what their words implied—a lift. "No thanks," I said, "I think I'll walk."

4

I WAS AVERAGING FIFTY-THREE MILES A DAY—THE PRECISE distance stagecoaches covered daily on their twelve-hundred-mile journey from New York to Savannah in 1802. (A ticket cost the then hefty sum of seventy dollars.) The hell-bent-for-leather cyclists I used to see training on the bike path back home would have considered fifty-three miles pretty wimp-ish, but I thought it was an impressive feat. My pale arms and legs were taking on a farmer's tan, my stomach felt firmer, though that may have been just wishful thinking. I liked the idea that my mind was on vacation and my body was now re sponsible for getting me through each day. I wasn't kidding myself, though. I hadn't set out to climb Mt. Everest or pad-dle alone across the Pacific in a canoe; bicycling solo across America is a low-risk, doable challenge. The fact that so many people I met thought it was an impossible undertaking per-haps had more to do with how little adventure and uncer-tainty they were willing to accept in their lives than it did with my own daring.

Route 231 to Charlottesville and then 250 to Waynesboro took me into the foothills of the Shenandoahs. My creaky knee had slowed my cadence to less than eighty pedal revolutions per minute, the number someone had told me was necessary to maintain a good pace. A Greyhound bus bound for Washington rushed by and I had a sudden unsettling thought: What if I simply decided that pedaling endlessly by day and seeking refuge in forlorn little motels by night was not how I chose to spend the next two or three months? What if in some town down the highway I simply got on a Greyhound and rode it home? I could tell my friends that my knee gave out, that I had had the heart but not the stamina. When people would ask if I'd made it to California, I'd joke, "Nah, I didn't even get out of Virginia." We'd laugh and that would be that. I couldn't get the notion out of my mind. The thought of home—Sandy, our two cats, dinner at the old pine table where years earlier her younger brother, now an attorney, had carved a dollar sign—was appealing. This could have been Rwanda, but it wasn't; I had choices. No one would accuse me of being a quitter if I had a legitimate reason for quitting.

A headwind came up. I was pumping hard but my speed dropped to nine miles an hour. I shifted into a lower gear and managed to go no faster. The general store in Shadwell where I intended to take my first coffee break of the morning had been thirty minutes away moments ago, when I was doing eighteen mph. Now it was an hour away. I was, in effect, going backward. For the first time in my traveling life, there was no predictable relationship between time and distance. My bicycle had both given me my freedom and made me a hostage. I rode on, through the Virginia horse country where farmland resembles lawns more than pastures and general stores serve espresso and sell *The New York Times* but not hardware. The houses were castlelike and occupied, in large part, by "Georgetown farmers"—people who had made their money in the city, or inherited it, and now lived as privileged country squires, at the end of long gated driveways that servants swept clean of leaves.

"This is your store? 'Cause if it is, I don't mean no disrespect standing here." The voice came from a big man with his left arm wrapped in a sling and it startled me as I walked out of the Shadwell general store with a cup of coffee. "You don't mind me waiting here for a ride, right?" he went on. "I'm trying to get home to the family reunion. We have it the first week of every September. Every year. I come down from Washington for it. Doing that for eighteen years. Only this time I'm staying. I'm coming home after eighteen years, back where I was born."

I explained that I had nothing to do with the store. Every now and then, when a car driven by an African-American came by, he'd dance out toward the highway, with extended thumb. The man looked vaguely familiar. I asked him where he had worked in Washington and he said, "I panhandled. Dupont Circle mostly, outside Chile Harold. Not a bad living at all. Those women, man, they loved me 'cause I was always respectful. That's the secret. They don't give you nothing, you just wish them a good day." Chile Harold was an honest saloon where I'd spent a few evenings. In fact I wasn't as far from home as I thought: I had regularly encountered the man who called himself Jiffy on the stoop outside the bar and remember him calling out to me, one evening when I walked by wearing an Orioles jacket, "Hey, if Baltimore don't get Chris Sabo for third, I'm giving up my season tickets." I turned back and gave him a buck. He hadn't lost his touch. Each customer who pulled into the Shadwell gen-

eral store in a big new car, he'd greet with a cheery "Mornin',
ma'am. Lovely day," or "Nice shoes you got there, sir. Get
them around here?" Most averted their eyes and walked into
the store without replying.

Jiffy said he had given up panhandling and was starting a
new career as a house painter. "So far, it's not going too
good," he noted. "I was painting a church and one of the
workers went crazy and hit me with a pipe. That's how I got
this busted arm." Still, he was happy to be back in the country because the city had worn him out, with cops hassling him
and drug dealers' bullets flying all over the place. "I got tired
of ducking," he said. I suspected Jiffy would do just fine in his
new setting and as I mounted up to leave, he asked if I could
spare two dollars for a pack of cigarettes. I said sure.

The next seven miles into Charlottesville, Jiffy said, would
be a good ride. He'd just hitchhiked over it and the road was
downhill all the way. "All you gotta do is coast," he said. So
I set off, knowing I had an uphill climb. I shared the road with
yellow school buses that lumbered over the hills. Produce
stands were selling the last fruits of the season, and I stopped
from time to time to snack on apples and melons. Cut hay lay
in the fields. Yellowed leaves skittered in my wake. The
towns were small and compact, places where neighbors knew
as much about one another as they did about their own families; I felt as though I were the only stranger for miles around.

Outside Waynesboro the road starts climbing. The grade is
steep, rising two thousand feet in two miles, and slows trailer
trucks—and aging bicyclists—to a low-geared crawl. With
each rise I shifted down, through all twenty-one gears until I
reached my granny gear, the lowest. My speed slowed to a
walking pace, four miles an hour, about as slow as I could go

and still remain balanced. I was pulling an elephant uphill, but I was making it, foot by foot, my butt pushed back in the saddle to gain maximum strength for each stroke. A car went by and the driver tapped his horn twice and waved. I focused on the pavement just ahead instead of searching for the peak and tried to imagine each stroke as a circle that involved lifting a pedal as well as pushing one down. That helped. I was soaked with sweat but not short of breath or unduly pained. Unlike headwinds, which can blow for days, mountains are only temporary inconveniences. They have a precise conclusion a set distance away—the summit—then grace you with a downhill run. I could conquer mountains but not headwinds, and when I made Waynesboro's peak at Rockfish Gap I pulled off the road to rest and to look back down what I had come up. The cars passed in a steady stream. Surely their drivers felt nothing at all upon reaching the summit, didn't even care that they were at the top. Yet the same accomplishment had elated me. That was the best thing about bicycling. It made special moments out of the routine and sharpened one's senses to the vicissitudes of travel.

My reward for making the summit was a straight shot into Waynesboro, three miles, all downhill. I biked the length of the town, looking for a saloon, but found nothing except a cluster of franchised restaurants. I didn't know it at the time, but I was entering a long stretch of dry rural counties that, with the exception of a couple of reprieves, would reach all the way into Oklahoma. I missed the congeniality of a good saloon. I found a motel room and nursed a cup of overheated coffee served from the lobby vending machine. My knee felt as if it needed a joint transplant and when I looked at the map of Virginia, I was surprised at how far I still had to go to get out of the state. The Greyhound kept popping into my mind. And so did Rosie Ruiz, the first woman to cross the finish line in the 1980 Boston Marathon. Rosie, a twenty-six-year-old administrative assistant for a precious metals trading firm, had come out of literally nowhere to win the race in what appeared to be record time for an American female runner. "How are you?" Bill Rodgers, the men's victor, asked her. Then he added, "*Who* are you?" The odd thing was that no one had seen Rosie at any of the checkpoints and her flabby thighs and full face seemed unlikely trademarks for a serious runner. It took a week for the truth to surface: Rosie had ridden the subway and slipped into the pack two miles from the finish line. She was, she said, just trying to draw attention to her fledgling acting career. She was stripped of her sapphire and gold medal. The last time I ran across her name in the papers was three years after the marathon, when she was arrested in Miami as part of an all-woman drug ring running cocaine.

I picked up the Waynesboro phone book and checked the listings under "G." I didn't, of course, really intend to do a Ruiz and ride the Greyhound a thousand miles, then claim to have biked the route. I just wanted to know what my options were.

5

THE NAME THOMAS STEVENS MAY NOT MEAN ANYTHING TO you. It didn't to me either until recently. But shortly after

getting the harebrained notion to bike across the country, I
grew curious about the history of bicycling and I found myself in the Smithsonian's stacks, poking through a wonderful
collection of books on the most arcane aspects of transportation imaginable. Tucked away on a top shelf, which I needed
a ladder to reach, was a two-volume set, published in 1887,
encompassing more than one thousand pages of text and en-
gravings. It was titled *Around the World on a Bicycle*—the
collected dispatches of Thomas Stevens's remarkable 13,500-
mile journey that began in Oakland on April 22, 1884.
Stevens was the first person to bicycle across the United
States, the first to bicycle around the world, and given the
condition—and absence—of roads in the country a century
ago, the account of his crossing is right up there with the adventures of Lewis and Clark for sheer daring.

Though the name Thomas Stevens was, briefly, once
known to virtually every American, his fame did not endure—primarily, I suppose, because we view the bicycle as
a recreational toy rather than a serious means of transportation. So unlike, say, the Wright brothers or Henry Ford,
Stevens wasn't seen as a contributor or trailblazer. He didn't
open the way for faster travel or more comfortable travel
or cheaper travel. All he did was prove that a man could go
coast to coast on a bicycle. Which is like saying all Neil
Armstrong did was prove a man could get to the moon in
a spacecraft. In reading Stevens's collected dispatches, one
is struck by his lack of self-absorption and the fact that he
pays scant attention to what motivated him to embark on
such an unlikely journey. In his time, when risk taking defined the national character, it was presumably not necessary, as it is today, to justify one's unconventional behavior

with a lot of psychological gobbledygook about midlife crises and career considerations and fulfillment of self. Just doing for the sake of doing was good enough.

Thomas Stevens was twenty-nine years old the morning he landed in Oakland, lugging his Columbia penny-farthing bicycle with a fifty-inch-high front wheel, on the ferryboat *Alameda* from San Francisco. His goal to cross the country by bicycle was one that seven others before him had tried and failed to complete. Born in England, he had migrated with his family to the United States as a teenager. He farmed in Missouri, tended store for a while, and wandered west to work in the Colorado silver mines and a steel mill in Wyoming. A small group of curious onlookers had gathered at the Oakland slip to bid Stevens Godspeed that April day and, wearing a baggy flannel shirt and trousers gathered at the knee like duck-hunting leggings, he mounted his bicycle and gave a wave with his broad-brimmed slouch hat.

"With the hearty well-wishing of a small group of . . . 'Frisco cyclers who have come, out of curiosity, to see the start," he wrote, "I . . . ride away to the east, down San Pablo Avenue, toward the village of the same Spanish name, some sixteen miles distant. The first seven miles are a sort of half-macadamized road, and I bowl briskly along."

One hundred and ten years later I was, in a manner of speaking, following his tire treads, though I am quite sure I would have given up quickly had I encountered the same impediments Stevens did. Finding no roads, he walked through sagebrush so thick he had to hold his seventy-five-pound bicycle overhead, and he rode along train trestles at one mile an hour. In a smoke-blackened tunnel cut into the mountains, he flattened himself against the wooden walls to keep from being crushed by a passing locomotive and taking refuge in a railroad snowshed in eastern California, he waited out the fury of a late-season storm. "Not a living thing in sight," he wrote, "and the only sound the occasional roar of a distant snowslide and the mournful sighing of the breeze through the branches of the somber pines, half buried in the omnipresent snow." In Nevada a mountain lion came after him and in Utah he stumbled into a herd of wild horses thundering down upon him on a narrow trail; he survived the cat by using his bicycle as a shield and the horses by firing his six-shooter into the air.

No matter how bad things got, no matter how grave the danger, Stevens pedaled on without complaint, never conveying the slightest hint of discontent or fearfulness. I suppose that was the difference between a true adventurer and a pseudoadventurer like myself. I was afraid of all kinds of things—heights, tightly enclosed spaces, deep water, bogeymen in the night. I needed a level of comfort, like a bed at day's end, and a standard of security, like avoiding roads that appeared on the map to be too isolated or too mountainous. I had limits. Straying too far off the traveled path unnerved me, while such transgressions invigorated Stevens. He crossed the rivers clinging to his bicycle and pieces of driftwood and made it over streams by using his bicycle as a vaulting pole. Cowboys mocked him and a band of Paiute Indians offered to swap a mustang for his strange-looking contraption. In Nebraska, where he passed homesteaders with wagons, tents and sod huts on the South Platte River, prairie winds blew him off his bicycle. "I consider it a lucky day that passes without adding one or more to my long and eventful list of headers," he wrote. In one Midwest town, an innkeeper turned him away for dinner, thinking he was a tramp.

Stevens arrived in Chicago on July 4 and rested for a week. He slept under wheat sheds in Cleveland and was arrested for riding his bike on a sidewalk there. In upstate New York, he followed wagon roads along tracks of the New York Central, then the towpath paralleling the Erie Canal. Mules bucked and snorted at the sight of him. The route was level, he wrote, but "the greatest drawback is the towing mule and the awful, unmentionable profanity engendered thereby in the utterances of the boatmen. Sometimes the burden of the sulphurous profanity is aimed at me, sometimes at the inoffensive bicycle, or both of us collectively, but oftener it is directed at the unspeakable mule, who is really the only party to blame."

By the time he made it to Boston on August 4, having covered 3,700 miles in 103 days, Stevens was a national hero, who had imprinted "the rubber hoof marks of the popular steed of the day" across roadless America. I would have quit right there, to bask in the adulation, but Stevens went on to bicycle across England, France, Germany, Persia, India and Japan. He was feted at receptions and given front-page coverage by American newspapers, which compared him to Jules Verne. A Turkish pasha said Stevens's journey was so extraordinary "America must build him a monument," and when Stevens tracked down Henry Stanley in East Africa on a subsequent trip, Stanley greeted him by saying, "You are Mr. Stevens, the bicycler who rode around the world, are you not?" Stevens's odyssey ended where it had begun, in San Francisco, in January 1887. He was hailed at a banquet in the Baldwin Hotel and honored by a poem:

And here's to Tommy's faithful steed
Who's where ever he'd roam,
Yet never failed him in his need
And brought him safely home. . . .

Not long after his triumph, the awkward "ordinary" or penny-farthing bicycle of Stevens's era—so named because the big front wheel reminded the English of a penny and the little rear wheel of a quarter-cent farthing—gave way to the "safety" bicycle we know today with a tubular steel frame, two small wheels the same size and a chain. Stevens's fame faded with the demise of the "ordinary." New adventurers headed off on safety bikes on even longer tours. When Stevens died in 1935 at the age of eighty-one, in a nursing home in his native England, his name had been all but forgotten in America.

6

AS FAR AS I COULD TELL, THOMAS STEVENS CARRIED NO maps and had no game plan. He simply went as far as he could each day. But I needed the security of a plan. Each morning I'd study my map over breakfast, stabbing carefully at a stack of pancakes so as not to slop artificial maple syrup over the route. Customers at the counter would often look over my shoulder and make suggestions on which I could not rely. My aim was to find a town that seemed big enough to have a motel and was far enough away to offer me an honest day's biking. Usually fifty or sixty miles was about right. In the East, where villages and towns are numerous and often within shouting distance of one another, this was easy. When I set off, I'd try not to focus on the destination, because fifty miles sounded too much like work, particularly if the roads were bad or the winds strong. Instead, I'd break the day into segments and view my eventual goal as a series of short rides. *Let's see, Vesuvius, that's about ten miles. I'll stop for a coffee break there. . . . Then I can shoot for Buchanan, another fifteen miles or so, and check out the town, maybe have lunch. . . .*

The orange marker line running southwest on my Virginia map called for me to leave Route 11 at Raphine and head off toward Rockbridge Baths on a narrow country road. But I liked 11, a highway that takes its time meandering from Rouses Point, New York, on the Canadian border, to the doorstep of New Orleans, and I decided to stick with it. The day was cool and in the towns I passed through kids wore their caps with the visor facing forward. John Deere was still a more popular logo in these parts than that of the Chicago Bulls or Malcolm X. Bib overalls had never gone out of style. Had it not been for the bum knee, I would have felt pretty good about the world. Aren't the legs the first to go when a body starts giving out? Remember Mickey Mantle's final days with the Yankees? He could still hit the ball a mile but his knees wouldn't carry him around the bases anymore. Maybe Mantle and I had both peaked. The road was flat and I shifted into my hill-climbing granny gear but managed to proceed at only a crawling pace. Every five or ten minutes I stopped to stretch and do deep knee bends. The knee would immediately stop hurting. Then I'd remount, pedal a few strokes and grimace. I began to think the problem was psychological—that mentally I wanted out of this adventure and my mind had induced pain to give me justification for quitting.

I had a bottle of Aleve, an over-the-counter painkiller, in my Ziploc shaving kit. I had used the pills after dental surgery a few months earlier, but it never occurred to me they might work on knees as well as teeth. "Give it a try," Sandy had said on the phone. "There's nothing to lose." It made no sense to me that a pill could be smart enough to know it is meant to attack the teeth one day and the knees the next. Still, I was willing to believe. I took a water bottle off my frame and held two pills at arm's length. "Now, listen up," I told them. "I want you to work on the *knees*. The knees, you understand? K-n-e-e-s." I washed them down with a gulp of tepid water, holding out little hope they would make a difference.

There was a café off to my right. I bought a copy of the local newspaper and went in. I asked where I could smoke and the cashier said, "Anywhere you like." I took a seat at the counter next to two farmers who were grousing about Public Enemy Number 1—the government in Washington. My paper reported that down the road a ways, in Back Valley, Tennessee, Dot Byrd's five-by-six-foot clapboard library was closing after thirty-eight years, to be replaced by a new community library in nearby Coalfield. Byrd was sixty-nine years old, a part-time nurse who received five dollars a month from the county as Back Valley's librarian. The library, topped by an American flag, housed two thousand paperback books and was open from 1 P.M. to 5 P.M. on Tuesday, though people were free to wander in any time to take a book because Mrs. Byrd never locked the door. Asked why she thought the library had become an object of national curiosity, written up by the *National Enquirer* and numerous other publications, Mrs. Byrd replied: "I have no idea. Like I told Johnny Carson, I thought he wasted his time having me come to California to tell him about the little library."

"What'll it be, dear?" the short-order cook asked. I already had had a big breakfast, so I ordered apple pie à la mode. She raised her eyebrows and asked if I wanted a side of baked beans too. I could not tell if she was joking or not. She had closed the café at midnight the night before and opened it at 6 A.M. and watching her at the grill was like seeing an artist at work. She had sixteen or seventeen orders going, the frying surface covered with French toast, pancakes, grits, hash browns, bacon, sausage, scrambled eggs, fried eggs and omelettes. She moved purposefully back and forth along the grill, flipping, stirring, stacking, filling oversized white plates with one order while reaching for the waitress's scribbled notations to start another: "Scram 2, bcn, HB, no tost, cfe, 2.99." I asked her if she ever fouled up an order. "Not often," she said. "Oh, sometimes I'll read a slip too quick and make a mistake, but the secret is all in the timing. You get a flow going. Your hands and feet sort of react automatically, like a dancer. You have to like what you're doing to do it well, and I love this. I've been doing it nineteen years and opening up the place every morning is still a kick."

"You take Edgar there," she said, nodding at the man to my right. "I start working his order as soon as he walks in the door. Two eggs over easy, biscuits and gravy, potatoes on Tuesday only. He's been eating the same thing for seven years. Maybe eight. I can tell you the eating habits of half the people in this town." Edgar did not respond to the mention of his name. He was engrossed in a conversation with Cecil, with whom he shared breakfast at the counter every Monday, Wednesday and Friday.

". . . So she was really trying to get off the dole, make something of her life," Edgar was saying, "but after three weeks she said, 'You know, I can't do this job. I'm better off on welfare. The benefits for the kids, the food stamps, I was much better off before.' So she quit the job and went back on welfare. That's the kind of system we got. The kind that won't let you escape welfare."

"That's the truth," Cecil said. "You get penalized for working. Now, you know my boy. He's a top student. There are 271 in his class and he's at the top. *The* top. He applied for a scholarship and you know what? He didn't even hear back from half the colleges. Know why? 'Cause I make over thirty thousand a year. That's the system again, and it all goes back to those people in Washington. They can't deal with any national problem. All they know how to do is keep themselves in office."

Edgar and Cecil were still swapping tales of injustice when I left. My bike was fastened with a coiled lock to a street sign at the curb. I unlocked it and started to push off. The wheels strained but didn't roll. I checked the front tire. It was fine. And the rear tire, it was . . . flat as a pancake. *Oh damn, now what happens?* I didn't understand why a tire would go flat when the bike was just standing there, going nowhere, and more to the point, not having changed a bike tire in forty years, I wasn't sure I was up to the task. My forehead dampened with sweat. I removed the rear saddlebags, set the bike on its side in the parking lot, and wrestled the wheel off the greasy chain, dirtying myself considerably in the process. The tire was surprisingly easy to pry off the rim. I replaced the punctured inner tube with a new one that I carried in the talcum-filled plastic bags. Bolts and valve caps and pressure gauges and tire levers were scattered on the pavement around me. "You look like you know what you're doing there," Edgar said when he walked by. "Oh sure," I lied, "I can change a tire in my sleep." I fumbled for twenty minutes trying to maneuver the rim by the chain and get the tire re-seated. Finally, on the umpteenth try, it slipped into place so easily I wondered what all the fuss had been about, and with my hand pump I managed to inflate the tire with 110 pounds-per-square-inch pressure—about 20 percent more than the recommended amount, because harder tires, though producing a rougher ride, create less rolling resistance, meaning you go farther with each stroke. It's a trade-off I'd make any time.

I moved back onto Route 11 gingerly, expecting perhaps I had messed up and would soon hear the dreaded *hissssss* of a wounded tire. No such thing happened. The rear tire was firm and stable. I felt extraordinarily clever. I followed the signs to Lexington and spent an hour biking slowly through the town, exploring this street and that. Stonewall Jackson, who was only thirty-nine years old when he died in the Civil War, taught natural philosophy for a decade at Virginia Military Institute in Lexington. His home remains, cared for and unimposing, at 8 East Washington Street and the entire town has the pleasing feel of a place that has been around for a while and matters historically. I left reluctantly, having found no affordable inn or motel, and was a good way down the road to Natural Bridge when I thought of my knees for the first time since I had taken Aleve.

Damn, what a bummer . . . Then it suddenly struck me: They didn't hurt! I pushed down hard with my right leg and "lifted" the other pedal with my left. Nothing. Not a twinge of discomfort. I braked, then accelerated as fast as I could. The knees did not balk. I let out a whoop. I had cured my knees and fixed my first flat, all in the span of an hour. The pills and I were miracle workers. I moved with a sense of mission, pedaling toward Natural Bridge at a brisk clip, and singing aloud the only song I know all the words to, "The Streets of Laredo."

7

ROUTE 11 FOLLOWED WHAT APPEARED TO BE A CUT IN THE mountains. The Shenandoahs were off to my right, small hills farmed with corn rose to my left. I had not seen another bicyclist since I left home, and I felt small and insignificant and very much alone as I made my way west. I had considered bringing a Walkman for company but decided not to because I wanted to hear traffic coming up behind me and the sounds around me. The decision had cut me off from all the "gray" background noise that is part of the cityscape, from the news and music and babble of voices that accompany us on the radio when we travel by car. What I heard instead was the wind, the soft, barely audible hum of my tires, a barking dog, a tractor coughing into gear. The sounds were new to me, different from anything I knew at home, and they reinforced my sense of being a stranger in an unfamiliar world.

I passed the miles talking to myself and, having been without company for quite some time now, found that I answered back. I saw stout, middle-aged farmers' wives and fashioned stories around what their lives were like when they were young and beautiful and full of dreams. I toyed with what I'd do if I hit the lottery. I had a gambler friend in Las Vegas who was always broke and I'd buy him a Cadillac. Beyond that I didn't have many imaginative ideas. I didn't want a bigger house or a faster bike. I never shop for clothes and the TV at home already brings in more channels than I know what to do with. The fantasy that sustains my lottery dreams is that money buys freedom, yet if anyone had freedom, I did, out here on the last days of summer, choosing any road on a whim, moving without timetables or due-dates. My freedom had come cheap, at about forty dollars a day, including room and board, and was a bigger prize than any lottery offered.

Over the years I have developed the peculiar custom of naming my appliances and vehicles, usually in honor of friends or passing strangers who struck my fancy. Among the occupants of my home are Tommy Toaster, Vicki the Vacuum Cleaner and Roberto the Electric Coffee Bean Grinder. Whitey, my red 1970 Buick Skylark convertible, is named for Bill White, a man with whom I spent an evening drinking martinis in a New York bar thirty years ago but have not seen since. The RV I lived in for five months while traveling the country and researching a book on minor league baseball was known as Forty-niner, commemorating what was then my age and my adopted state, California. I would not have considered setting off on the baseball journey in an unnamed RV. All this came to mind as I poked along Route 11 and realized that not only was my bicycle without a name but that I had no intention of giving it one. As best I could figure, here's why. Whitey and Forty-niner had been, in a manner of speaking, both companions and bodyguards on long journeys. I could ride out storms in them, lock their doors and feel secure in them, count on them to get me where I wanted to go if I fueled them, bathed them, and cared for their squeaks and groans. But my bicycle was only an extension of me. It was like another set of feet. It couldn't carry me anywhere I didn't have the endurance to go; it couldn't protect me from danger or keep me warm and dry when the weather turned nasty. So I came to view my nameless bike as a device whose elegance lay in its simplicity but one that wasn't a companion any more than were my legs. I'd look at the bike parked next to my bed when I awoke and feel dumbfounded that anything so uncomplicated, so relatively cheap, so undemanding could carry a person across a continent, or around the world. My bicycle rose to meet me at my level of expertise and in return asked for almost nothing: no fuel, no oil, and if I was lucky, little maintenance for thousands of miles, except to lubricate the chain every couple of weeks and after every rainstorm. In an age of waste and extravagance, the bicycle is of the future. It is inexpensive, nonpolluting, and more efficient than any form of self-propulsion ever devised. A one-hour trip by car, for example, burns up an average of 18,600 calories; the same one by bicycle uses 350. Those monster steam engines that pulled freight across the country after World War II needed seven thousand horsepower to maintain their pace; even a lawn mower needs a horsepower or two; my bike, gliding along Route 11, past farmhouses where couples sat in rockers on their lawns, surrounded by an odd assortment of unwanted possessions from scrub boards to stacks of *Saturday Evening Posts* they offered for sale, needed only one tenth of a horsepower to get me to my destination.

In Buchanan, Route 11 becomes Main Street. I biked the length of it, then doubled back and stopped in front of the state liquor store. I had left my bottle and my book at home to reduce my load but I had grown accustomed to the weight of the saddlebags and another pound or two wasn't going to make much difference. Weight, in fact, becomes a factor on a bicycle only when accelerating or climbing. It doesn't affect your speed once you're rolling on a level road. I hadn't seen a bookstore in a single town since leaving Alexandria, so I couldn't do much about my lack of literary stimulation, but a solution was at hand for the loneliness of shabby motel rooms. I bought two pints of Canadian whiskey and tucked them in the rear saddlebags. I now had a good incentive to have a drink: Each one would lighten my load. The clerk called after me, "Don't forget to get a designated driver," and laughed so uproariously that I, missing the humor, felt foolishly somber.

I left my bike unattended and walked a couple of blocks along Main Street. Buchanan was a quiet town, neither dying nor prospering. Many of the stores were empty, having succumbed to nearby Interstate 81, which had sucked businesses out of downtown and into a new commercial core closer to the highway. The family-owned jewelry store remained—jewelers are always the last to give up on the old downtown—but the movie theater was shuttered and I couldn't

find a coffee shop or a drugstore. When I asked a local
whether Buchanan had a store that sold books, he replied,
"Doubt it very much. You'd probably need to go to
Roanoke for specialty items like that." I had never thought
of books being *that* exotic and wondered exactly what kind
of book he thought I was looking for.

The only town of consequence between Buchanan and
Roanoke is Troutville. It was marked with red letters on my
AAA map, leading me to believe it might provide food and
shelter. I covered the fifteen miles to Troutville with little effort, rolling easily over the gentle hills, unaware of either any
pain in my knees or the extra weight in my saddlebags.
Troutville straddled Route 11 but appeared so small I had to
ask in town hall where the main part of the village was. "This
is it," the clerk said. "This is all we got." There wasn't much
more than a few shops covering half a block. I asked what
went on in Troutville. "Used to be a steel plant down the
road," she said, "but that's closed up now. To tell you the
truth, we don't do much here at all anymore." I hung around
for an hour anyway, talking to the waitress in Fletcher's Grill
about the weather and the local high school football team,
and watching two men from the volunteer fire department
put a spit-polish shine on the town's fire engine. Like most of
the towns on this once heavily traveled route, Troutville had
an air of vanished prosperity. It was almost as if these communities were marking time, daring the fates that had claimed
so much of Main Street, U.S.A. They no longer offered a
refuge to the traveler because the hotels and restaurants and
gas stations had closed and relocated along the ramps of interstates. Even the downtown barbershops and hardware
stores were disappearing, and in their place stood tanning sa-

lons and video stores. The transition saddened me. For a person rooted in the city, I had always felt strangely at ease in Small Town America, but moving through it now on a bicycle I saw something I had not seen before from a car's window: the horizon of isolation. It was a spiritual, not geographical, thing, and it moved with me down the road, through each little town where the young men were gone and the women who stayed behind had grown plump, and, even in the best of times, scratching out a living was a hard day's work.

8

I MADE MY WAY INTO ROANOKE AND WAS SURPRISED HOW pleasing it was to be among tall buildings and crowded streets again. Traffic on Orange Avenue was heavy and moved fast, but I wasn't spooked the way I had been on Route 1 in Fredericksburg. I waited in lines of cars when lights turned red, took left turns on green arrows without eliciting angry honks and maintained enough speed on the straightaways so as not to annoy anyone. All in all, I felt no more out of place heading across Roanoke on my bicycle than I would have in a car. I stumbled upon a bookstore and chose Michael Shaara's Civil War novel, *The Killer Angels*. In an ice cream shop, I ordered back-to-back chocolate milk shakes and drank them so fast that I had to muffle a burp. I found a vending machine that sold *The New York Times* and a bicycle store where I bought an inner tube to replace the one that had gone flat near Cloverdale. Seldom had life been so full of exciting choices.

It had been a couple of days since I had considered turning back. Rosie Ruiz and the Greyhound had not even entered my mind since Waynesboro. The aches I felt were no longer painful ones. They were the aches of muscles tightening and dormant body parts awakening. My stiff-legged walk had the feel of a purposeful swagger. The accomplishments of each day were clearly measured now in miles traveled or hills conquered, and I liked having such a simple yardstick to judge success. At home I could spend a full day laboring at the computer over a few hundred words that were entirely unsatisfactory. With a keystroke I would wipe them from the disk, and the blank, blue screen would stare back, a reminder that the day had slipped by as a dark, empty void. On the road there are no such voids. I had only to examine the map to find tangible proof of daily achievement. With each inch the miles from home grew greater. It was like bricking in your backyard. You always knew exactly what you had done and what remained.

Normally I wasn't particular where I spent the night, and when there was a choice to be made, price was usually the determining factor. But I had decided to take a day off in Roanoke and if I were to spend two nights in the same motel, I had some special requirements. There had to be a laundry nearby, and a restaurant and grocery store. I needed a phone jack in the room so I could use my computer modem to get messages. Cable TV and a close-in saloon were pluses but not essential. Free coffee in the lobby was more of an enticement than the availability of a swimming pool. Single-story structures—or at least a room on the ground floor—were non-negotiable so that I wouldn't have to lug my bike up a flight of stairs. I considered a deluxe room not one with a king-size bed but one large enough to turn my bike around in.

In the week since leaving home, I had covered 250 miles, not a great distance, really, yet long enough to make me feel smug that I had gone so far in so short a span. If I had quit back in Waynesboro, I might have been forever reluctant to take on crazy new challenges. The boundaries of age would have been set. How odd it would be if this journey changed my life and turned me into a true eccentric who thrived on jumping out of airplanes and taking on the toughest white-water rapids. "Where's Lamb? I haven't seen him for a while," someone might ask, and Sandy would say, "Oh, he's walking the Appalachian Trail." Highly unlikely, I realized, yet the thought that I had embarked on an odyssey that might turn my life in an entirely new direction was exciting. I also realized I was not a person who did unusual things merely to privately relish the glow of self-satisfaction. The reaction of friends was important to me. I needed recognition, needed to hear confirmation that I lived beyond the perimeters of the ordinary. That was my insecurity: What I wrote became good only if someone praised it and where I biked became noteworthy only if someone said, "Amazing. I couldn't have done that."

Except for my nightly calls to Sandy—in which my conversation was laced with enigmatic jargon about headwinds, potholes and rough shoulders—I had not called any friends, nor had I sent any postcards, and when strangers asked my destination, I usually replied, "I'm hoping to get to California," with the emphasis on *hoping*. Though quitting now seemed out of the question, I hadn't convinced myself yet that the Pacific really was within reach. The Oklahoma Panhandle, the Rockies, the Mojave—they seemed insurmountable obstacles, and so much unknown territory lay between me and the West Coast that I wondered if at some point my body would rebel or my spirits flag upon being asked day after day to perform beyond their limits. I wasn't sure what might derail me. The weather. The mountains. An accident. Loneliness. They were all potential enemies and I decided it wise not to call any friends until I had crossed a border of no return.

I passed a Marriott and a Hilton and had a pang of fondness for the days when I traveled the country on an expense account and never thought twice about what a hotel room or a meal cost. But spending my own money, instead of the boss's, was a different kettle of fish and I got antsy if my dinner tab topped seven or eight dollars and a night's lodging came in at over twenty-five dollars. These were easy boundaries to stay within and I had forgotten how inexpensive life along the highway is when the dinner menu doesn't include wine and no chocolates grace your turned-down bedcovers I continued on through Roanoke to Salem and when ahead I saw Interstate 81—six lanes that run from the Canadian border near Watertown, New York, to the outskirts of Nashville—I knew I would find a refuge for the budget-minded traveler. Six or seven motels were clustered near one of the interstate ramps and I chose the one that advertised the cheapest rooms—thirty dollars for a single—on its marquee.

"Any discounts?" I asked the clerk. "Corporate? Triple-A? Commercial?"

"No. Just AARP. But you don't look old enough to be retired."

"How about a discount for bicyclists?"

"That's never come up before. But sure, why not? Twenty-five, plus tax." It seldom failed. I could almost always knock a few dollars off the price just by asking. I was not a skilled bargainer—even when I lived in Egypt, I usually ended up paying full price in the souk—but trying to reduce my lodging costs became one of the little mind games I played to break the tedium of travel. Upon entering a motel, I'd immediately size up the clerk, ranking him or her on a scale of one to five: One meant the clerk was going to be a cinch for a reduced rate, five that I'd have to pay full price or walk. Women were usually fours or fives and far more unyielding on the price than men.

Although my wardrobe was small, I had to wash my clothes in two loads in order to avoid being naked in the laundry room. First I changed into my street clothes and dumped all my biking gear into the washer. Then I changed back into my shorts and jersey and washed the street clothes. Finally I got back into my chinos and sport shirt. It was a laborious process but I felt invigorated to be in clean clothes. I decided to lighten my load and mixed a drink. I connected my Toshiba to the phone jack and dialed up my message basket in the *Los Angeles Times* computer in L.A. It was empty. I resisted the temptation to send any messages to friends. Instead I opened up my journal file and started typing in the day's update: ". . . Did fifty miles today. Taking two Aleve pills every morning and knees feeling good now. Just ahead are Appalachians which look very tall and reach westward in a series of layers that seem to go on forever. I wouldn't mind having company going up into the mountains but haven't seen another bicyclist since I left home. . . ."

9

TAKING A DAY OFF WAS REGENERATIVE. I SLEPT LATE, ATE A big breakfast and had nowhere to go. Although I had taken an unpaid leave of absence from the *Los Angeles Times* to make my journey, the paper's editors had agreed to buy an occasional article about the crossing on a freelance basis and the Voice of America wanted a biweekly phone call from me, which would be broadcast around the world on its English-language service. I figured the proceeds from these two assignments would just about cover my expenses for the entire journey. More important, they legitimized the trip in my own mind: If I were earning an income and practicing my trade as I went, I had purpose; I was more than a dilettante in flight from middle-class responsibility. By midafternoon I had filed my story to the *Times* and called VOA in Washington for a five-minute Q and A. I wondered what someone in, say, Kenya or Tanzania would think of my journey. To Africans, and to most of the Third World's people, a bicycle is a badge of poverty—a vehicle of last resort for those who cannot afford a car—and the idea that anyone might choose to get on a bicycle and bike three thousand miles for the hell of it would be incomprehensible. But rather than thinking me quite mad, I hoped foreign listeners would realize that my trip was symbolic of something important in the United States— the extraordinary freedom we have to move. We can venture down any road, poke through any town and never encounter a roadblock or anyone in uniform who will turn us back. That may seem pretty basic, but in Africa, where I had lived for eight years, I visited countries like Ethiopia and Zaire where people couldn't leave their neighborhoods without government authorization and any journey down a rural road almost surely meant getting stopped by drunken soldiers and shaken down for money. To wander across an entire continent and never need a visa, never be in danger, never hear an unfamiliar language (though the Virginia drawl did at times sound foreign) would be, to many Africans, beyond the realm of believability.

I was eager to get going again after being stationary for a day and I headed out of Salem and into the mountains at first light. The road rose and fell like a roller coaster. I hugged the white line, focusing on the pavement twenty yards distant rather than trying to search out the summit. The sun moved overhead and the day turned warm. Sweat dripped into my eyes, ran down my legs, soaked through my just-washed jersey. The ice in my water bottles melted. My speed dropped, six miles an hour . . . five . . . four. I stopped and sat on a guardrail and gulped half a bottle of warm water. *God, if these are only the Appalachians, how do I get over the Rockies?* The Appalachians are a biker's downfall. They seemed to come without warning, just when I was flying along, thinking all the world was flat, and the roads up them are straight and steep, like a staircase to the clouds. They test your mettle like nothing I had experienced before.

Back home when I ran into a hill of consequence, I either went around it or turned back. Never did I go over it. But then, my training techniques were suspect from the start. Rather than getting into condition by tackling varied terrain on increasingly long training runs (everything I read about training advocated grueling routines apparently designed to make biking as unpleasant as possible), I had set off ill prepared and let my body work itself into condition on the ride. It wasn't a fashionable way to go about things in the Jane Fonda era of no pain, no gain, but it worked. Actually, the one day I attempted a serious training ride had turned into something of a disaster. I set off on my bike for the Ashby Inn in Paris, Virginia, seventy-five miles from home. Sandy drove up in the afternoon, with plans that we would meet at the inn for dinner about seven o'clock. The first fifty miles were over the abandoned Washington and Old Dominion Railroad track bed, which had been turned into a bike path. I covered them with energy to spare. In Purcellville, the path ends and I swung onto a two-lane country road that snakes over a long chain of undulating hills. The sky darkened, rain swept across the meadows in driving sheets, thunder and lightning cracked overhead. Having no rain gear and no warning lights, I took shelter with my bike under a giant oak (the most dangerous thing I could have done with lightning around; I should have hunkered in a ditch, away from my bike). It was nearly dark when, struggling up another hill, splashed by car after car that sped past with headlights ablaze, I heard a beep, beep. I knew without even looking back that it was Sandy and she had rightly figured I needed rescuing. She pulled off the road just ahead. The bike rack was on the back of her station wagon and I, a defeated man, needed no encouragement to lift my bicycle onto it and drive the final eight miles to the inn, shivering and sneezing all the way. I suspect if I had heard Sandy's horn while pushing over the Appalachians I would have once again gladly accepted liberation.

At least now, though, on Route 11, heading for Pulaski, the weather was cooperating. I had not seen a drop of rain since leaving home. There were storms to the south and floods to the north and I had found a patch of sunshine and was following it right across Virginia. Foolishly, I had left my wet-weather gear at home, and I prayed my good fortune would hold until I made it over the Rockies, where autumn snowfalls are common.

Pulaski's streets glistened with recent rain but the sun was out when I arrived at the downtown square. I had missed the storm by an hour. The town, named for Count Casimir Pulaski, who was killed during the siege of Savannah in 1779, has a population of ten thousand. Under the elm trees that line Washington Street are plaques, each bearing the name of a deceased local resident. Four dollars in the Golden Steer restaurant gets you a six-ounce hamburger steak, gravy, potatoes, unlimited salad and dessert. There's a bar in the motel outside town but it's open only on weekends. I have never seen anyone, even the banker or the mayor, wearing a coat and tie in Pulaski.

Five years earlier I had spent ten days in Pulaski, researching my book on minor league baseball. It was a grand time and the RV I lived in that summer offered a luxurious lifestyle compared with my present circumstances. I set up camp, so to speak, outside the two-thousand-seat Calfee Park, where a few feet from my door the Pulaski Braves of the Appalachian League treated me every evening to baseball as it was meant to be—a game played on real grass, in the intimacy of a small park, by young men who dared to dream and were not yet spoiled by fame or fortune. I befriended the Braves' manager, Fred Koenig, a fifty-eight-year-old baseball lifer whose wife followed the team bus to every road game in her Chevy van, and I remember taking pitcher Mark Wohlers and several teammates to lunch at the Golden Steer. After wolfing down everything in sight, Wohlers, a teenager who then played for little more than meal money and would go on to become a star reliever for the Atlanta Braves, asked me: "Can you get free seconds on the pie?" So Pulaski held good memories for me, and although the minor season was over and the major leagues were on strike when I came through town on my bicycle, I was curious how baseball and Pulaski had fared in the years that I had been gone.

Four firemen and a couple of rescue-squad volunteers—all with suspenders and substantial girths—were standing outside the fire station. They pretended to ignore me when I pulled up. People often did that but were usually eager to talk, which they did easily after I broke the ice with a question about their town or the road ahead. I asked directions to the motel, then inquired about the fate of the Pulaski Braves.

"Danville got 'em," one of the firemen replied, referring to a town near the North Carolina border. "They built 'em a new stadium and the Braves, they just picked up and moved Course, we're trying to get a new team. I suspect we will, 'cause we got a ball field and this is good baseball country."

I had not forgotten the way to Calfee Park. I biked up a steep hill and turned onto a road that led through a neighborhood of small clapboard homes whose porches were stacked with firewood. Calfee Park sat at the end of the road. I peered through its locked gate and felt a touch of melancholy: The team had moved away, Fred Koenig had died of a heart attack the previous winter and who knew how long the wooden bleachers reaching down the first and third base lines would remain empty? The Braves had averaged the smallest crowds in professional baseball—389 a game—but Calfee Park had been a fine place to spend a summer evening. When I looked across the wet, unmowed field I could hear the echo of voices and all but see Koenig bent over in the third base coaching box, hands on knees, head upturned toward home plate. Had Forty-niner, my old RV, been parked outside the gate, I would have happily scrambled aboard and settled in to rediscover a game that only a few middle-aged diehards like myself still dare call our national pastime.

10

THERE ARE 3,380,000 MILES OF ROADS IN THE UNITED States and it didn't take me long to figure out that none of them were designed with the bicyclist in mind. As often as not potholes, broken glass and hazardous sewer covers obstructed curbside lanes where I rode, and Route 11's shoulder, when one existed, was graveled, which would have sent me flying had my wheels strayed onto it. I could imagine an engineer at his drafting board in Richmond growling, "Ha! Those *bastard* bikers! I'll get 'em. Look at this: If we gravel the shoulder here we'll get some beautiful headers, and up here, where the traffic gets heavy, we'll make the shoulder disappear to scare the shit out of them." It worked. I seldom let down my guard or lost my concentration on what my wheels would pass over ten or fifteen yards ahead. *Lord, give me a shoulder to ride on.* All I wanted was eighteen inches of smooth pavement to drift away from the stream of traffic. It didn't seem an unreasonable request.

In the town of Chilhowie ("Valley of Many Deer" in the language of the Occaneechis) a young man on the sidewalk caught my eye as I pedaled slowly by and said, "Good luck." I felt a kinship with him, knowing he understood that my mission was difficult and solitary. Chilhowie had been established in 1750, when a frontiersman named Samuel Stalnaker built a cabin along a stream in the empty valley. The little Virginia settlement that followed became part of what the colonies then referred to as the "Far West." Like most outposts of the era, it lay near a well-traveled Indian path—one that in time would become a crude road known as the Wilderness Trail (which in 1774 Daniel Boone widened while in the employ of the Transylvania Company), then Route 11.

By the time the white man arrived, North America already was crisscrossed by thousands of miles of trails, usually on high ground and along ridges, seldom more than two feet wide, because Indians traveled single file and found that elevation provided safety from forest fires and enemies, as well as a good place to view game. Among the early thoroughfares were the Occaneechi Trail running south from Virginia, the Chickasaw Choctaw Trail through Tennessee, the Iroquois Trail from the Hudson River to the future site of Buffalo, Nemacolin's Path (named for a Delaware Indian) from the Potomac Valley across the Alleghenies to the confluence of the Allegheny and Monongahela Rivers, where Pittsburgh now sits. The trails followed routes of convenience, avoiding swamps and using gaps through mountains, for instance. As Philip Mason points out in his book *A History of American Roads,* the network of paths grew over time into the United States's modern-day highways and railway right-of-ways and influenced the location of many major cities: Boston, Buffalo, Newark, Albany, Pittsburgh, Detroit, Chicago, Omaha, Kansas City, St. Louis, Louisville, Cincinnati, Denver and Santa Fe.

Considering the desperate condition of those early roads, I should probably temper my complaints about a few potholes. Of New York City's streets in 1892 Rudyard Kipling wrote, there were "gullies, holes, ruts, cobblestones awry, kerbstones rising from two to six inches above the level of the pavement; tram lines from two to three inches above the street level; building materials scattered half across the street; lime, boards, cut stone and ash barrels generally and generously everywhere." Rutted, muddied or flooded roads between towns were often impassable, hindering the ability of farmers and manufacturers to get their goods to market. Stagecoaches got stuck, and passengers were expected to debark and push. In the 1830s—when 80 percent of the United States's population lived east of the Allegheny Mountains and the nation had 27,000 miles of "roads"—novelist Caroline Kirkland described her stagecoach reaching a mud hole in the Middle West:

> *The driver stops, alights, walks up to the dark gulf and around it if he can get round it. He then seeks a long pole and sounds it, measures it across to ascertain how its width compares with the length of his wagon. If the hole is less than three feet deep, the driver is happy.*

"The roads of the United States are inferior to those of any civilized country," Professor William M. Gillespie of Union

College in Schenectady, New York, observed in the mid-1800s. Charles Dickens would have agreed. Visiting Ohio before the Civil War, he set off in a stagecoach early one morning, luckily in high spirits.

It was well for us, that we were in this humour, for the road we went over that day was certainly enough to have shaken tempers that were not resolutely at Set Fair, down to some inches below Stormy. At one time we were all flung together in a heap at the bottom of the coach, and at another we were crushing our heads against the roof. Now, one side was down deep in the mire, and we were holding on to the other. Now the coach was lying on the tails of the two wheelers, and now it was rearing up in the air, in a frantic state.

Although the National Road from Cumberland, Maryland, to Wheeling, West Virginia—the first state-to-state road built with public funds—opened in 1818, not until the 1880s did an organized effort to improve the quality of the nation's roads begin. The protagonist was an unlikely one: the "wheelmen," as cyclists were then known. The bicycle had been introduced to the United States on a wide scale in 1877, when Albert Pope, a former Civil War lieutenant colonel, converted an old shoe factory in Hartford and started building the first American bikes. They cost $313 each and weighed seventy pounds. Within a few years touring became wildly popular, but the bicyclist's lot was not a happy one. Seated precariously over the man-high front wheel, he (women who rode bikes then risked being branded immoral) pitched headfirst over the handlebars when the road became rough. Angry equestrians whose horses bolted at the sight of bicycles cursed the cyclists and stuck sticks and riding crops in their spokes, causing yet more headers. Many cities, considering bicycles a menace to pedestrians and horses, banned wheelmen from streets and parks (including New York's Central Park). Some cities taxed bicycles, in the form of a registration fee. Haddonfield, New Jersey, refused to let bikers use its "turnpike," which was nothing more than a crosstown road used by horse-drawn vehicles.

In the summer of 1880, a group of frustrated cyclists formed the League of American Wheelmen (LAW) in Newport, Rhode Island, to "ascertain, defend, and protect the rights of wheelmen, to encourage and facilitate touring. . . ." Enthusiastically supported by Pope, the organization lobbied state legislatures and got antibicycle ordinances overturned. It provided funds for the legal defense of cyclists sued by farmers and teamsters who said bicycles had frightened their horses, causing overturned carts and runaways. It published maps that listed hotels, road condition and other vital information otherwise unavailable in an era before road maps. The league's most important program, started in 1888, was to educate the American public about the advantages of improving the nation's roads. With more than 100,000 members, including many prominent citizens such as Andrew Carnegie, John D. Rockefeller (who one year gave bicycles to thirty-eight overweight friends), and Diamond Jim Brady (who gave his girlfriend a $10,000 gold-plated bicycle with mother-of-pearl handlebars), LAW sponsored "good roads" meetings and conventions throughout the country, distributed millions of pamphlets detailing highway problems, ran candidates for public office on a "good roads" platform, was responsible for the placement of the country's first road signs and eventually convinced leery taxpayers that roads should be improved not for the pleasure of cyclists but for the economic welfare of the nation. By 1890, LAW had a chapter in virtually every town big enough to have a hotel. Brooklyn—the first city to construct a path exclusively for bicycles—was soon to open the five-mile-long Coney Island Cycle Path, and Seattle had set aside more than twenty miles of bike roadways on which carriages were banned.

The league faded quickly when, with the advent of the horseless carriage, the bicycle boom died. The road was about to be transformed from merely a means of getting from here to there to a metaphor for a lifestyle. In 1903—when the United States had 17 million horses, 10 million bicycles and 23,000 cars—H. Nelson Jackson and Sewell Crocker left San Francisco May 23 in their two-cylinder, twenty horsepower, open-air red Winton. Using many wagon roads and railroad rights-of-way, just as Thomas Stevens had on his bicycle nineteen years earlier, they reached New York in sixty-three days to become America's first transcontinental motorists. Nine years later Carl Graham Fisher, an auto-parts manufacturer and founder of the Indianapolis 500, began advocating the construction of a 3,389-mile highway from New York City's Times Square to Lincoln Park in San Francisco. Named the Lincoln Highway, it would be the country's first coast-to-coast road. The era of scientific road-building was about to begin.

LAW went out of business in 1942 due to public apathy, but was reborn in 1965 following a resurgence of bicycling in the country. Now headquartered in Baltimore and known as the League of American Bicyclists, it operates as a nonprofit advocacy organization with more than 24,000 members, 500 clubs nationwide, and a network of thousands of member homes where long-distance bikers can stay for free. As I headed out of Virginia, praying for a shoulder or even a curb-side lane free from shattered beer bottles, I made a mental note to send the league a donation as soon as I got to California.

11

I CROSSED INTO TENNESSEE JUST BEFORE NOON, ON A SUNNY, windless afternoon, ten days and 402 miles from home, and let out a whoop that must have echoed to Knoxville. If some-one had told me a year ago I was capable of *bicycling* clear across Virginia and into Tennessee, I would have dismissed him as loony. Though it was not my intent to become a phys-ical fitness freak, I had to admit I did feel shockingly fit. My shorts no longer cramped my waist and the shape of my legs had changed as muscles hardened and bulged. Let's see: The doctor wanted to put me on medication because of high cho-lesterol; everyone said I was doomed if I didn't swear off to-bacco, alcohol and fast foods; friends found a thousand reasons why I'd fail. I was too old ("Are you the oldest man ever to attempt this?" an interviewer had asked me in Wash-ington, D.C.). I was out of shape. I hadn't trained. I didn't know how to repair a bike. I'd go nuts with loneliness. I'd de-hydrate in the desert. I'd collapse on the plains, get snow-bound in the mountains. The doubters were my inspiration.

I could hear the echo of their voices every day calling, "Turn back. Turn back." Their concerns, of course, had crossed my mind too from time to time, and I wanted nothing more than to prove to them—and myself—that even a middle-aged reprobate with bad habits could have a life.

"There's still no way Dave can make it all the way across," a friend who can find gloom in the brightest spring morning told Sandy the day I got to Tennessee. "After two weeks everything will start to break down. The legs. Lungs. Spirit. His butt will feel like a pincushion and his arms'll be as inflexible as steel pipes. California? No way."

Sandy replied: "I don't think you know Dave. When he makes up his mind he's going to do something, he does it. I suspect he'll make it even if he has to walk over the Rockies."

At home Sandy was besieged by phone calls from friends inquiring about my whereabouts. Her solution to keep from repeating herself so often was to change the recorded message on our answering machine each day: ". . . Leave your message after the beep. And if you're calling about Dave's bicycle odyssey, on Saturday he reached Kingsport, Tennessee, 422 miles from home." When I called home and got the machine instead of Sandy, the confirmation of progress always gave my spirits an uplifting jolt.

The moment I crossed the state line, a wonderful thing happened: Route 11 widened. Hurrah for Tennessee, a pox on Virginia. I was now riding a well-paved shoulder, five feet across, no longer dodging traffic and potholes. For the first time I owned a secure little chunk of highway. It was *mine*. My grip on the handlebars relaxed. My shoulders sagged, rather than hunching up around my neck, as though someone had massaged knotted muscles. Never in a car had

I even been aware whether a road had a shoulder, and now having that extra lane was about the most important thing in my life. There probably wasn't another person within five hundred miles who thought a good road shoulder had anything to do with happiness, but a simple truth had become evident to me the past few days: It is the little things over which we have no control that often carry the most weight in making each day a pleasure or a burden.

Two flat tires—my fourth and fifth of the journey—within the span of an hour did not undermine my good spirits. I set up shop at the farthest edge of the shoulder and worked, I thought, quite nimbly with my patch kit. It was odd that I should be undone by a smooth roadway, but I noticed that a dozen spokes had lost their tension and become wobbly. I ran my finger along the inside wheel rims and found several other spokes whose heads were rubbing against the inner tube. With underinflated tires, the errant spokes are like pins touching a balloon. I had avoided using air pumps at gas stations to keep my pressure up because the sudden explosion of air is so powerful it can blow a bicycle tire off the rim. But I pledged to be more attentive in checking pressure and to use my hand pump nightly, even though it took an Olympian effort to reach a level of 110 pounds per square inch by hand.

In the Tri-Cities yellow pages (for the life of me I couldn't figure out what two cities joined Kingsport to make up the "tri-cities"; my map didn't show any other sizable metropolitan areas within a two-day ride), "bicycles" fall between "Bibles" and "billiard equipment." Under bicycles, there was a listing for a place called Larry's, the only bike shop for miles around. I called. On the wall next to the phone, just outside the men's room of the bar, was a vending machine, identified as a "Convenience Store," which sold nothing but hangover remedies and the most diverse assortment of condoms I'd ever seen: condoms that glowed in the dark, condoms imprinted with the American flag, condoms with ribs and nipples and lubricants. Larry finally answered. I said that I needed to have my spokes adjusted and to get a Mr. Tuffy protective rim liner, something I shouldn't have left home without. But Larry was closing up for the day and wouldn't be open Sunday and I didn't feel like weekending in Kingsport. He said my wheels would probably hold up for the hundred miles or so to Knoxville, a university town with several bike shops, and I moved on.

It was a good decision because I liked Bean Station, the town I ended up in for the night. Bean Station was at the intersection of Routes 11 and 25 and had the only motel between Rogersville and Knoxville, the Harris Motor Court. A flashing neon arrow pointed to the one-story brick structure. Painted within the arrow were the words ELECTRIC HEAT. The motel had a large, empty parking lot, an unfilled swimming pool and a 120-seat restaurant with, at the moment anyway, no customers. A handwritten note taped to the door of the motel office said, FOR ROOMS, INQUIRE IN DINING ROOM. There wasn't much else around except the Bean Station Diner down the road and a row of stores, most of them boarded up, and the highway was quiet save for an occasional eighteen-wheeler rumbling through town on the back roads to Spartanburg, South Carolina. I half expected to see a portrait of President Eisenhower on the diner wall and to pick up a newspaper and find out Casey Stengel was managing the Yankees and the French were bracing for an assault on Dien Bien Phu.

"The motel's been here fifty years and I've been here half of 'em," the waitress in the deserted dining room said. "We're both getting old together. I guess I'll just stay till I die." She said Bean Station had been a bustling place before the interstate came through a few miles away, and she could remember when eight waitresses worked the floor and the dining room stayed open until midnight. Now it closed at seven, sometimes earlier if there were no customers, and she was the sole guardian on this shift, serving as both waitress and cashier. The ham was still cured in a local smokehouse, though, the chili was fried in an old iron skillet and the pies were baked fresh daily. I asked her how the town had gotten its name and she reached behind the cash register and gave me a photostat copy of Bean Station's history from a Tennessee newspaper. The print was so small and smudged I had to put on my reading glasses. "That'll be fifteen cents, please," she said.

It turned out that Daniel Boone and a man named William Bean had come here in 1775 and, near an Indian warpath along a ridge to the east, bought thirty-eight acres for $16.75. A few years later William's wife gave birth to a son, Russell, the first white child born on the Tennessee frontier. Russell Bean matured as an unruly lad and, shortly after marrying, set off one day in a flat-bottomed boat on the Nolichucky River with a cargo of arms he had manufactured. When he returned two years later, he found his wife nursing a child not of his making. He was so infuriated that he got drunk and cut off the child's ears to mark him as illegitimate. Bean was arrested and sent before the traveling magistrate, who sentenced him to jail and ordered that he be branded on the hand. While in jail, Russell Bean bit off the brand.

I finished the afternoon snack—banana cream pie and fried onion rings—and told the waitress not to close up early: I'd be back before 7 P.M. for dinner. She gave me a key to Unit 12 across the parking lot and said I could settle up in the morning. My day's end routine was well established now. I washed my biking clothes and hung them to dry on a barb-wire fence enclosing a cow pasture, just behind the motel. I showered, rubbed the plum-red seat sores on my butt with Vaseline, and changed into street clothes. I called Sandy and we chatted about the smallest daily details of both our lives. I mixed a drink from the bottle in my saddlebags and sat for an hour with my computer on my lap, writing the day's journal. I spread maps on the bed to study tomorrow's route. I pumped up my tires, checked the chain, examined the taut-ness of the brake and derailleur cables. The routine took a couple of hours. I had worked up a good appetite by the time I returned to the restaurant. It was 6:45 P.M. The din-ing room was empty and the waitress said, "I was wondering when you'd show up. I kept the place open for you."

12

"YOU AND YOUR BICYCLE ARE ONE OF THE STRANGEST things to come through town but not the strangest. The strangest was a man on a packhorse two years ago. Right after the big blizzard. He was going coast-to-coast. He asked if he could camp out back, and I said, 'Course you can.' He spread out his sleeping bag, rubbed down the horse and gave him some oats, built a fire to cook his dinner right over by the big oak. It was quite a sight. I said to him, 'Don't you worry, being out alone on the highway? There's so much meanness in the land now.' He said no, the thought of personal safety never crossed his mind.''

The woman shook her head in disbelief. "Jean," she said to the waitress, "you can reach for that coffeepot whenever you got a chance." The breakfast crowd had come early to the Bean Station Diner. The woman and I were at the counter and she had struck up a conversation after seeing my bicycle leaning against the window outside and picking me out as the probable rider. I was easy to identify: No one else was wearing shorts, a jersey with three pockets on the backside and silly-looking stiff-soled biking shoes; besides, I was the only stranger in the place. "Meanness in the land." I had never heard that phrase to express the fears awash in America. Violence. Drugs. Gangs. Those were the operative words. But *meanness* implied something had gone awry in the national character. It referred to attitude as much as to behavior. The notion that a basic change had taken hold in the United States was an unsettling one—and one I heard uttered over and over in back-road towns from Virginia to California. People worried they were no longer immune from the ills of our cities. They worried that their insular communities were easy prey for strangers in an increasingly mobile society. They worried about the randomness of violence, and the more they worried, the less safe they felt. No one in the diner could remember the last time Bean Station had had a robbery or a serious crime. ("Miss Anita's lawn mower was stole last summer, but I guess that don't count," one man said.) Still, the perception of violence was all about them. They saw it on television every night, they read about it in city newspapers. They probably knew a local boy who had gotten in trouble with the law. This was not the world they had grown into a generation or two before, when strangers helped strangers and went on their way with a tip of the hat. *Meanness* might have been used in those days to describe the temperament of the town bully, but not the disposition of a nation.

The diner was small, with four tables and half a dozen seats at the counters, and after a while everyone was engaged in a single conversation of sorts, with a farmer by the cash register adding comments about the horseman who had passed through and a trucker at the far table shouting out questions about my journey.

"Can I ask you something personal?" he said.

"Sure." The diner fell silent, awaiting the question.

"How many miles a day can that thing do?" He waved his hand toward my bicycle outside.

"Well, *it* can do about a thousand," I said. "But *I* can only do fifty or sixty." He thought about that and nodded.

I hung around the diner, talking and smoking, for a couple of hours and it was later than usual, about 10 A.M., when I finally got rolling. Half a dozen customers came outside to see me off for Knoxville, fifty-four miles away. "I sure don't envy you, but travel safe," one said. The farther from home I had gotten, the more I was viewed in these little towns as an oddity, like some dispossessed traveler from another age. People gathered around my bike in parking lots and general stores, asking what was in my saddlebags and where I slept at night and how I figured out a daily route. "What's your wife say about this?" they'd inquire, or, "How'd you get the time off from work? You look too young to be retired." What seemed to intrigue them most was that I was making the journey alone. Didn't I know the highways weren't safe anymore? When I'd ask, "Well, is it safe around here?" and they'd say, "Oh, sure, you won't have any problems here," I would reply, "That's what they say everywhere I've been. So I figure my odds are pretty good of not running into trouble." Rather than being reassured, people often seemed disappointed that I didn't have a prime-time TV horror story to share.

I made good time getting to Knoxville. There was not a breath of wind, and the wide shoulder on Route 11 was as good as having my own private bike path. I stopped on Court Street in Rutledge to examine the replica of the tailor shop Andrew Johnson shared with the sheriff in 1826. Remarkable, I thought, that an apprentice tailor—a former indentured boy at that—could become president of the United States. But was it any more remarkable than a peanut farmer or a movie actor becoming president? Farther down the road, I pulled into a graveled turnout where an elderly man from Kentucky and his wife had set up a flea market next to their van. "Gas money is about all we get out of this, and a chance to keep moving," he said. Laid out on the ground near the van were used jigsaw puzzles, pieces of pottery, kitchen gadgets, a few well-worn tools, stacks of old *National Enquirers*. The man offered to give me the *Enquirers*, but I told him I couldn't take on any extra weight.

His wife looked at my bicycle and said, "My son had a motorcycle too. He was killed on it, three years ago next Tuesday. You know Ray Perkins's garage? It happened right there, by the bend. A man in his car, turning left, hit him. You never get over something like that, try as you might. That's when we started driving around, right after the funeral."

Though I didn't attempt to clarify whether her son had been on a motorcycle or bicycle, I had no doubt about the dangers of traveling on two wheels. Fifteen hundred bicyclists a year are killed in the United States, and over six hundred thousand injured. Of the fatalities, 96 percent involve a collision with a motor vehicle and 75 percent are the result of head injuries. Not an hour went by that I wasn't aware of my vulnerability, and without realizing I was even doing it, I had developed a list of survival techniques. There were the obvious precautions, of course: wearing a helmet, going with the traffic (not against it as bicyclists did when I was young), riding predictably. But most important was striking a balance between being assertive in staking claim to a thin ribbon of blacktop and being the most timid guy on earth, willing to yield to the whims of drivers who had the ability to squash me like an ant. *Yes, sir, you come right on by. This road is all yours. I won't be any bother at all.* When trucks came up behind me on a shoulderless road, I stopped pedaling and coasted to the right until they passed. This served a dual purpose: It let the driver know I was aware of his presence and it confirmed I did not intend to challenge him. Grateful truckers blinked a thank-you with their marker lights after they had passed and pulled back into the lane. I dealt with motorists prepared to nudge onto the main road from a side street by establishing eye contact and staring them down until I was safely past. That way there was no question who was claiming the right-of-way. My biggest threat came from RVs, whose drivers were usually elderly and indecisive, and from trucks hauling timber and coal, whose drivers weren't much more than metal-to-the-pedal short-haul cabbies. I had good luck with most motorists in cars, but as a group, only the long-distance truckers—or OTR (over-the-road) truckers, as they're known in the transportation industry—seemed not to want me dead and gave me the respect a bicyclist needs to survive.

I made Knoxville by midafternoon and crossed town on a congested, high-speed parkway that I would have avoided had I not been trying to find a bike shop before dark. Interwheel Sports was located a few blocks from the University of Tennessee, on a nondescript street where almost every store had hung a banner rooting on the Tennessee Vols. (I asked if a Vol was some kind of Southern bird or animal and was told no, the football team's nickname honored the state's "volunteers" in the Civil War.) The young mechanic in Interwheel put my bike up on a rack after I had removed the saddlebags. He squeezed several pairs of crossed spokes that had become as flexible as rubber bands and said he was surprised my wheels hadn't "collapsed." I shuddered at the thought. He worked for a couple of hours, trueing the wheels and putting tension back in the spokes, while I sat in the corner, on the wooden floor, drinking Dr Pepper and reading USA Today. My bill was sixty-eight dollars. It was the only bike expense I would have on the entire journey. Figuring it's about three thousand miles between coasts, that meant the bare-bones cost of crossing the country on a bicycle was a little over two cents a mile.

13

I CANNOT PROVE THIS, BUT I BELIEVE TENNESSEE HAS MORE dogs per capita than any other state and most of them are ornery. For bicyclists, they are the curse of Tennessee. Unfenced and untethered, they chased me from border to border. Dogs as big as bears and rat-sized terriers, dogs with throaty growls and little pests with high-pitched yelps, dogs in packs and snarling beady-eyed loners apparently in need of a good feed—I encountered them all, and had I brought a gun along I would have been tempted to leave a trail of carcasses across the entire state. One group would pick me up at the edge of a farmer's property and pursue me to the perimeter of the adjoining farm. There, another group, alerted by the barking, would give chase to the next fence line, stopping abruptly the moment I was out of their territory. They seemed to pass responsibility for hunting me on up the line, like I was some kind of wild animal to be chased down until I dropped from exhaustion. The wiliest curs would come up silently from the rear and suddenly appear behind me as a team, some closing in from the left, others from the right. My acceleration was phenomenal in these moments of panic. I'd throw my entire body weight onto the pedals and, even on a hill, manage to double my speed, or so it seemed, in a few pedal strokes, actually outracing my tormentors until they grew bored with the hunt and turned back, panting and wagging their tails. Luckily, most of Tennessee's dogs are dim-witted, and, instead of running diagonally across a field and trying to cut me off, would come straight at me, leaving open my high-speed avenue of escape. I became the victor so often that my fears diminished.

Dogs have given me a fright ever since childhood, when a Saint Bernard mistook me for a rabbit and forced me up a tree, and before heading for California, I sought the advice of several cyclists on how to deal with canine encounters. No two offered the same counsel. Among their suggestions: Turn your bicycle around and chase *them;* thump their skulls with your air pump; yell in your most authoritative voice, "No! Go home!" (dogs, being dumb, will think it's their master's command); squirt them with your water bottle; dismount and place your bike between yourself and the attacker; let out a bloodcurdling scream as you were taught to do during bayonet training in the Army; pray. For me, the best approach seemed to be the "No! Go home!" command combined with prayer and the fastest speed I could muster. But I intended to leave nothing to chance. When I heard barking or approached an unkempt house—generally the more run-down the house, the nastier the dogs that lived there—I took the pepper-gas canister from the mesh pocket on the outside of my handlebar bag, put my index finger on the trigger and rode ready to fire.

On a long rural stretch between Knoxville and Rockwood, I passed one of those dilapidated houses with a junked-up frontyard and suddenly, as though someone had opened the door of a kennel, sixteen or seventeen howling curs bolted out of nowhere. Feet churning, bellies low to the ground, they closed in on their target—me. My cadence increased so rapidly my rear tire nearly burned rubber. I was yelling "Go home!" and wildly firing the canister over my shoulder when the fastest of the lot pulled alongside. He was a black mongrel, about two feet high, with no collar, and the pepper-gas spray hit him squarely in the snout. He bolted upright as if someone had yanked furiously on an imaginary leash, hit the ground and whimpered. I glanced back. The pack had stopped short and was milling about the fallen mongrel in stunned confusion. I sped away and didn't stop to let my heart calm down until I was over the next hill.

After Farragut Route 11 branches left at a fork, heading south toward Lenoir City and Sweetwater. I kept straight, tracking a westward path. Eleven had been my companion for more than a week and I left it reluctantly. There is a sense of comfort and security in sticking with one road, not having to worry about missing turns or taking shortcuts, going wherever it goes, and had it continued in the right direction I would have gladly followed my newfound friend all the way to California. The pavement narrowed on Route 70, my new way west. The countryside became dark, almost foreboding. Deep forests pushed to the highway's edge and in the glades stood wooden sheds where stalks of tobacco dried. On tree after tree small hand-lettered plaques, as abundant as the Burma Shave signs that once adorned the nation's highways, declared: JESUS IS THE ANSWER, TRUST JESUS, LOVE JESUS, PRAY TO JESUS, STAY SAFE WITH JESUS, EMBRACE JESUS. It was hard to go more than a few miles on the empty road without passing a Baptist church. Ahead loomed an unnamed mountain that I hadn't spotted on the map. The road to the summit was five miles long, straight up and over. Including rest stops, the climb took me over an hour, and by the time I reached the peak I looked as though I had emerged from a shower. Three old men in plaid shirts and overalls were sitting on tree trunks at the top where the road leveled out. Their presence surprised me because I hadn't seen anyone at all, save a few passing motorists, for most of the morning. A basket of apples and a pile of watermelons were stacked near the roadway, next to a cardboard sign that said, FIREWOOD FOR SALE. One of men was whittling a chunk of oak with his pocketknife.

"What are you making?" I asked.

"Nothin'," he said. "I don't make nothin'. I just whittle."

We fell into conversation. Dale, the oldest of the group at eighty-six, had lived all his life in the Tennessee hills around Eaton Crossroad. Mostly he had farmed tobacco, for decades with two teams of mules, but three years ago his brother had been killed in a tractor accident and Dale said he hadn't cared much for farming since. In his childhood the nearest public road was ten or twelve miles away. Then in 1937, Route 70 was built. "It was dirt, and it used to do a horseshoe right around the hill over there and follow the creek. Oh my, come spring, the cars'd be stuck in mud up to the top of their wheels. I remember my brother and me hauling my old Ford—it was a 1923 model, I believe, and it cost me four hundred dollars, new—out of the mud with the mules." He gave my bicycle an admiring look and asked what I had paid for it. "I hate to admit it," I said, "but about twice what you did for the Ford." He spat a stream of tobacco juice and said, "Suppose you gave all that money to the Japs, too."

"Nope. My Trek's American-made. Waterloo, Wisconsin. Friends who know a lot more about this stuff than I do tell me it's the best touring bike you can buy." I didn't add that my tires were from Germany, my inner tubes from Taiwan, my gears from Japan, my saddle from Italy, my shorts from Korea, my windbreaker from Hong Kong, my biking gloves from Sri

Lanka. Dale said he still had the first bike he had ever owned and asked if I wanted to see it. He walked the hundred yards to an old, tottering barn identified by a sign over its door as ORAY'S ELEGANT JUNK SHOP and a moment later came riding back on a rusty, clanky bike, circa 1920, a mischievous smile stretched ear to ear. Next to my Trek, with its dropped handlebars, cantilever brakes, and bar-end shifters, his bike looked like something out of the Middle Ages. "If you want company," Dale said, "I'm ready. Truth is, I always dreamed of going to California. Used to think about it a lot and figured one day I'd get there for sure, but I never did and now I'm too old." He paused for a moment and added, "Now, ain't that sad."

Rockwood, a four- or five-hour ride away, was identified on my AAA map in small, black letters, which was a bad omen for finding a place to spend the night. The small letters indicated the town didn't have much of a population and might be a motel-less way station, and black, rather than the more reassuring red, meant that the American Automobile Association had found no lodging or dining facilities worthy of recommendation. I headed there anyway, arriving at dusk. The road went through town in a straight shot, four lanes wide. I stopped at the first gas station to ask if Rockwood had a motel and the attendant said, "Yup, there's one a mile west, but I don't imagine you'll much like it. Last I heard it was bought by foreigners." The Indian couple who ran the motel charged me twenty-two dollars and said they could not discount what was already a bargain rate. They gave me a tray of ice from their refrigerator, fixed my sluggish air conditioner and drove me in their car the mile to Junior's, Rockwood's only restaurant. Pork chops, three vegetables, rolls, salad and coffee cost $3.59. I left a dollar tip and thought the waitress was going to kiss me in gratitude. It was 8 P.M. when I left. Junior locked the door behind me, and I stepped out onto a deserted street. In the windows of shuttered stores neon lights blinked. Nothing moved on the single train track that cut through town and there was no sign of the Greyhound that stopped twice a day on the Nashville–Knoxville run. I sat for a while on a bench in the little park Rockwood had built for the bicentennial, hearing the labored breathing of Small Town America, and let the darkness settle in. All that was familiar had slipped out of my life, leaving me in a world of quiet isolation. Walking back to the motel, I passed a row of homes hardly larger than miners' cabins. Dogs growled in the night and on one porch I could make out the outline of a woman sitting in a rocker. "Evening, ma'am," I said. She did not answer and I wondered if she might be dead. I walked on. Once home, I spent an hour cleaning my bicycle with a roll of the motel's toilet paper, scrubbing off the dirt until the bike looked shiny new and as roadworthy as a Peterbilt eighteen-wheeler.

14

THE CHALLENGE WAS NO LONGER PHYSICAL. IT WAS MENTAL. My body had started to respond obediently, like a machine, pedaling on and on, day after day, week after week, through valleys, across plains, up hills. It did whatever it was told to do. Bicycling six or eight hours a day was simply what I did, as much a part of my unthinking routine as riding the Metro to work had once been. But my mind still balked at leaving the security of a motel room. Each morning a quiet sense of fear gripped me. It was a fear born of the unknown, of being alone, of seeing zero daily miles registered on my odometer and knowing I had so far to go.

Actually, making the journey alone had never been part of my plan. But a friend who was going to come along awoke one morning a few months before our planned departure and realized he had no more interest in biking to California than he did in walking to the moon. "I like the idea of finishing," he said, "not the idea of getting there." Another friend, a photographer, signed on and almost immediately was shipped out on assignment to Africa. I skimmed the classifieds in several bicycling publications and found that bikers were in demand. "WANTED," an ad would say, "experienced cyclists for Los Angeles–Boston. Leaving early July. Mostly camping, some motels. Share costs, cooking duties. Average 120 miles a day." I envisioned strangers arguing over whose turn it was to cook and whether to knock off for the day at the camp ground in Monteagle or Boonshill and decided that a cross-country bike trip was probably the wrong place to make new friends. So in the end I had the choice of putting the trip on hold or going it alone, and putting life on hold is something you can do when you're twenty, not fifty-four.

Never did I regret the decision. The nightly phone call to Sandy was all I needed to overcome brief twinges of loneliness and my aloneness bothered me only in the abstract. I could bike when I wanted, rest when I wanted, quit for the day when I wanted. I alone determined how many miles I would go, where I would stay, when I would eat. I could take a leak along the side of the road and blow smoke rings in my motel room without apologies. My days were marvelously self-centered. I had been freed of responsibilities, of conversations not of my choosing, of all goals, ambitions and missions except to reach a destination. At times I questioned whether I could ever comfortably rejoin a structured society.

In previous wanderings through America I often wondered why I seldom saw truckers reading newspapers when they stopped for meals and now I knew the answer. The highway is a cocoon and life beyond it does not seem to much matter. The highway has its own rhythms, its own inhabitants, its own codes of behavior. It is a world unto itself, egalitarian and isolated, and to be a citizen of it one has to have only the need to keep moving. The drivers I saw in truck stops, eating chicken-fried steak and drinking coffee by the thermos, were self-absorbed, as happens to everyone who surrenders his life to restlessness. They had their logbooks to fill out and maps to study and calls to make to dispatchers in Savannah and Houston and Minneapolis. There wasn't time for things that had no impact on the road ahead.

Before leaving home, I spent some time researching the evolution of our road system and was surprised to learn that were it not for the Conestoga wagon, we might still be following the British pattern of driving on the left-hand side of the road, as we did in the first few decades of nationhood. Drivers of the Conestoga—or prairie schooner, as it was known during the settlement of the West—were stationed on the left of the wagon, walking, riding the lazy-board or astride the near wheelhorse. To have a clear view over six horses and a wagon that spanned sixty feet, they found it necessary to keep their vehicles to the right. Soon other carriages and cargo haulers were following in the deep ruts cut by the wagons, and in 1813 New Jersey became the first state to order wagons to stay to the right.

For the next hundred years or so, America's roads were not part of a national system at all. They were a patchwork of rough corridors that occasionally ended at county lines, and more often than not varied in width and quality when passing from one jurisdiction to the next. In an effort to give the network some order, Congress passed the Federal Highway Act in 1921, demanding road continuity as a requisite for federal aid, and in 1925 the secretary of agriculture approved the Uniform System of Numbering. North–south roads received odd numbers, with the Old Post Road along the Atlantic becoming U.S. 1 and the westernmost road skirting the Pacific assigned the highest number, U.S. 101. East–west roads got even numbers, from U.S. 2, which links Houlton, Maine, with Everett, Washington, to U.S. 90, which runs across Texas. *The New York Times* lamented that the numbering system would rob the open road of its romance: "The traveler may shed tears as he drives the Lincoln Highway or dream dreams as he speeds over the Jefferson Highway, but how can he get a 'kick' out of 46 or 55 or 33 or 21?" Though motorists may have dreamed less, they soon were navigating the country on two-lane roads, paved and numbered, and they lined up by the hundreds the day the Pennsylvania Turnpike opened in 1940 to take a spin on the nation's first four-lane, divided superhighway. "The American's road system can now take him to every place in the land worth going to," *Fortune* magazine said. The 160-mile-long turnpike, from Carlisle to Irvin, followed the right-of-way of the unfinished South Penn Railroad and had no speed limit. It was the first American highway better than the cars it served.

Roads ran from town to town through the forties, but in

1958, in recognition of the revolution that automobiles had wrought, the federal government began building the townless highways that had been first proposed during the Roosevelt administration. The interstate system—45,000 miles of transcontinental roads, 53,000 bridges, at a cost of $129 billion—was the largest public works program in history. "Coast to coast without a light," the early PR literature promised, and Americans loved the idea. Twenty years later the final stretch of I-90, from Boston to Seattle, was completed near Blue Lake, Minnesota, and painted gold, in a ceremony reminiscent of the Golden Spike that marked the opening of the transcontinental railroad. "Red-Eyed Pete"—the last stoplight on the interstate system—was removed in 1984 near Caldwell, Idaho, placed in a coffin and buried. The serendipity of road travel would never again be quite the same.

Bicyclists are allowed to ride on some interstate highways in the East with special state permits (and can ride them in only a handful of Western states), yet I considered myself fortunate to be traveling a route that still went town to town. Near the Natchez Trace Parkway a highway sign welcomed me to Deerfield and, though I saw nothing but a Baptist church there, another sign a few hundred yards down the road thanked me for visiting. In Lawrenceburg, where Davy Crockett had lived and run a gristmill until he got into a squabble with the county commissioners and took off for the Alamo, I read a classified ad in the local newspaper that said: "Notice to anyone who bought a Fender guitar from North High Pawn Shop. I'd like to buy it back. Great sentimental value." Tullahoma was cutting down a red oak that had stood on the ground of the civic center since before the Civil War. Spring City, which houses its chamber of commerce in a red caboose, was trying to raise sixty thousand dollars to save its old train depot. Frankewing (marked on my AAA map with small black letters) had given up and turned into a ghost town. Except for one ramshackle store that sold groceries, antiques and deli sandwiches, the whole place had moved a mile west, to huddle near an exit ramp on Interstate 65, which links Chicago and Mobile.

The cotton that sustained this stretch of Tennessee until the turn of the century had given way to fields of tobacco, corn and beans. The mountains were fierce, coming in layers one after another, and on Jasper Mountain a line of cars stacked up behind me as I struggled toward the summit at a snail's pace. No one honked, no one shouted obscenities. I moved onto the dirt shoulder and stopped to let the motorists go by. The lead car pulled alongside and stopped too. "Go on," the driver said. "You got here first." Dumbfounded, I struggled on. At the top of Jasper Mountain the road flattens into a long, level plateau that runs for seventeen miles. The caravan of cars sped by me. Drivers waved. I swung into a general store, bought a quart of chocolate milk and sat on the stoop, next to the pay phone, map unfolded, trying to decide whether Route 64 or the more northerly and rural 199 was the best way to Bolivar and Memphis. Two men got out of a muddied pickup. "Mind me asking where you're going?" the tall one said. He was bearded and wore boots and had a wide leather belt with a silver buckle as big as a dollar bill. I pegged him as a trucker. Sixty-four was the best route to Memphis, he said. No question about it. But how was I planning to get across Arkansas? I fished around in my saddlebag until I came up with the Arkansas map. I opened it up and laid it out on the ground, adjoining the Tennessee map. He nodded but made no comment on my choice of routes. Had I given Oklahoma much thought? he asked. And what about

New Mexico? Soon I had six state maps laid out, border to border, in the windy parking lot, their edges held fast by pebbles. The maps stretched for perhaps fifteen feet and the man—who had retired from a lifetime of trucking two years ago and said he knew every road worth knowing in the country—walked the length of them, studying the orange-marker line that reached from Bristol to Los Angeles. "Here's what I think," he said, tapping a closed fist against his jaw in concentration. "They got you going way too far north, three or four hundred miles too far north. You're going to run into snow, ice, bad cold up there this time of year. What you want to do is drop south. Head for Oklahoma City, not Tulsa. Then I was you, I'd take this sucker right here." His finger followed Route 60 from Amarillo to Phoenix. "It'll add 122 miles to getting to the coast but it'll save you grief weatherwise. I'll tell you this, though. That mountain you just came over is the worst one you'll find till Flagstaff. Oh, they'll tell you they got mountains in Arkansas but don't believe them. All they got over there is little bitty mounds. Here to Flagstaff, it's all pretty much downhill."

The thought of dramatically altering my route made me uneasy, because the orange path across the United States was my lifeline. It told me where I was going tomorrow, and the day after, and in doing so, it removed some uncertainty from the journey. But I took encouragement from what my friend said about the mountains. If I really had just taken on the baddest of them, what was there to stop me from getting to the West Coast? That night, for the first time, I wrote half a dozen postcards to friends. Instead of saying I was *hoping* to make it to Los Angeles, as I had said to strangers en route early on, I said California was within reach, five or six weeks away, and my progress was steady.

TWO

ACROSS THE MISSISSIPPI AND THE OKLAHOMA PANHANDLE

*Life is either
a daring adventure,
or nothing.*
—HELEN KELLER

1

IN 1966 THE MONKS OF GROTTOFERRATA, NEAR ROME, working on the restoration of Leonardo da Vinci's manuscripts, came upon a rough sketch, probably drawn in the 1490s, of a bicycle. It was an eye-catcher because the bicycle didn't exist, even in its crudest form, until about 1815. Though the sketch was not a da Vinci, the artist may have been one of his students, the monks reasoned. But it did confirm the obvious: that for centuries man had dreamed of finding a machine that would beat walking. The bicycle was the perfect answer. And who gave us this gizmo that enabled us to go faster and farther under our own steam than ever before? Actually, no one man invented it. Rather, the bicycle evolved in Europe, slowly by trial and error, during the nineteenth century. A German was the first to attach two wheels to a wooden support with a handlebar and a seat. A Scottish blacksmith figured out how to make the vehicle self-propelled with a set of foot-powered cranks. A French cabinetmaker came up with the idea of pedals. What emerged by the mid-1880s pretty much resembled the bicycle we know today. In the 175 or so years the bicycle has been around, American inventors have made only one contribution to its basic design: the fat-tired mongrel known as the mountain bike, which Gary Fisher, tinkering with parts of motorcycles and tandem bikes in his California garage, developed in 1974. Within a generation, along with hybrids or cross-purpose bikes, it would account for nine of every ten bicycles sold in the United States. Touring bikes like my graceful, thin-tired Trek 520 were soon to become an endangered species.

Historians trace the genesis of the bicycle to Germany, where in the 1810s Karl von Draise, groundskeeper for the Grand Duke of Baden, developed a hobbyhorse-like contraption: The rider sat astride a plank connected to wheels at the fore and aft and propelled himself by walking. Draise used his "draisienne" or "walking machine" to inspect the duke's forests. In 1818 he sent his forest huntsman to Paris to put the draisienne on public display for the first time. The day did not go entirely well. The huntsman was taunted by children, a bystander grabbed the draisienne and tumbled off trying to ride it, a crucial assembly bolt was lost, and at least once the huntsman had to get off the vehicle and push. The demonstration was canceled. Nevertheless, Draise eventually left the duke's employ to devote full time to marketing his invention, to which he added an upholstered seat, luggage rack and cord-operated brake. (He died impoverished in 1851, at the age of sixty-six.) Though the draisienne was probably the fastest vehicle in the world at the time and was briefly in vogue in Europe and the United States, it didn't really work very well: It couldn't go uphill, it had no traction on wet roads and its lack of suspension made riding uncomfortable.

Designers in Europe started fiddling. Kirkpatrick MacMillan, the Scottish blacksmith, displayed his self-propelled crank-driven two-wheeler in 1839 and beat a carriage in a race. In the early 1860s, Frenchmen Pierre Michaux and Pierre Lallement unveiled a new model with an iron frame, wooden wheels and pedals. The velocipede or boneshaker, as it was known because of its rough ride, cost three hundred dollars and weighed more than a hundred pounds. Velocipedes were introduced in the United States in 1868 and, like the draisienne, briefly found an audience. Riding academies sprung up in America's Eastern cities and Harvard students rode boneshakers on moonlit nights along the Charles River. In Troy, New York, they rented for twenty-five cents an hour. Said the *Federal Republican and Baltimore Telegraph:* "A curious two wheeled vehicle called the velocipede has been invented, which is propelled by jackasses instead of horses."

Despite widespread ridicule, the English continued to refine the two-wheeler. To increase speed the front wheel became larger, until it was as tall as a man. The wooden frame gave way to steel; tires of solid india rubber were added. These high-wheelers were called wheels, bicycles, ordinaries or, derisively, the penny-farthing, and though difficult to master and so dangerous to ride that "Death by Bicycle" columns started appearing in U.S. newspapers, they signaled the birth of America's generation-long affair with the bicycle. In his 1884 essay "Taming the Bicycle," Mark Twain wrote that it took him eight days to learn to ride without having an instructor alongside on foot to balance his high-wheeler. "It takes con-

siderably longer than to learn horseback-riding in the rough,"
he said. Each day's lesson lasted ninety minutes and although
he wrote that he could have learned without a teacher, "the
self-taught man seldom knows anything accurately, and he
does not know a tenth as much as he could have known if
he had worked under teachers; and, besides, he brags, and this
is the means of fooling other thoughtless people into going
and doing as he himself has done." Among Twain's proudest
achievements was learning how to avoid dogs.

About this time, in the mid-1880s, John Starley of Coven-
try, England, started making a "dwarf ordinary" or "safety"
bicycle with a tubular steel frame, a chain, two thigh-high
wheels roughly the same size and a seat that could be raised
or lowered. In 1887, while toying with his son's tricycle, John
Boyd Dunlop, a Scottish veterinary working in Belfast, got
the idea of filling a bike's tires with air to smooth the ride,
something that had been tested unsuccessfully on horse carriages forty years earlier. Thus was born what we ride today—
the "safety" bicycle with pneumatic tires. Its use became so
widespread in the United States that some people spoke of
railroads becoming antiquated as a form of public conveyance
and Thomas Edison predicted that hundreds of miles of cycle
paths would be constructed and equipped with overhead cables to supply power to electric motors mounted on bikes. In
1896, more than four hundred companies in the United
States were manufacturing bicycles and mass production enabled Wanamaker's in New York City to offer one model for
sale at $27.50. A competitor, the Siegel-Cooper Department
Store, countered with a $22 bike. Wilbur and Orville Wright
put a price of $18 on the bikes they made, about the cost of
a ready-made suit. "The cycle trade is now one of the chief

industries of the world," noted the February 1896 edition of *Outing,* a popular magazine about travel and leisure activities. The next year bike sales in the United States topped two million. On the bicycle assembly lines, manufacturers were drawing the blueprint for mass production that Henry Ford (who was a skilled bicycle mechanic) and others would bring to the auto industry a few years later.

The early automobile, in fact, relied on technology developed for bicycles. As Leon Dixon, founder of the National Bicycle History Archive of America, writes, shaft drives, gearing, differentials, detachable pneumatic tires, wire-spoke wheels, even semiautomatic transmissions were widely or at least experimentally used on bikes long before anyone ever built an automobile. Even the early car makers had links to a bicycle heritage: Chrysler's Dodge division started as a company that manufactured Evans & Dodge bicycles; Pierce-Arrow motorcars descended from Pierce bicycles; Cadillac and Lincoln grew out of the Leland-Faulconer Company, which made special bearings for chainless bikes; Thomas Jeffrey made bicycles before he began manufacturing the Rambler car, as did North Willys before making the Overland; Albert Champion, for whom A.C. and Champion spark plugs are named, was an early bicycle racer.

None of this has much to do with getting from Virginia to California, except that, in a way, my journey had become a history lesson, introducing me to a chapter of travel lore that I had never given thought to. In town libraries along the way I would check the card catalog under "bicycles," and although the category was often blank, I did find some wonderful nuggets, which I would dutifully type into my computer.

I read about Fanny Bullock Workman, daughter of a Massachusetts governor, who spent the years from 1889 to 1902 on her Rover bike pedaling through Europe, Africa and Asia, dressed in Victorian-style high-neck blouses and billowing skirts that concealed her ankles. To ward off dogs, she carried a steel-cord whip with six wire barbs attached to the business end. "One blow was usually sufficient to change the barking into a short, sharp yelp," she wrote.

One book I found introduced me to Marshall Walter Taylor (1878–1939), a onetime Indianapolis errand boy who endured constant racial discrimination to become America's top bicycle racer—and the second African-American to be champion of a U.S. sport. (Bantamweight boxer George Dixon was the first.) Though crowds loved Taylor, other riders threatened his life and often tried to run him off the track. In Minneapolis a white rider choked him into unconsciousness. Some publications suggested Taylor was somehow responsible for the violence. "The position of the Negro is a trying one," said *Bearings* magazine in 1897, "for every rider is anxious to top him, owing to his color, and the battle to beat him is waged fiercely day by day." After winning the one-mile world championship race in Montreal in 1899, Taylor stood as 12,000 Canadians cheered him and the band played "The Star-Spangled Banner." He later wrote: "I never felt so proud to be an American before, and indeed, I felt even more American at the moment than I had ever felt in America." Taylor retired from racing in 1911, at the age of thirty-two, and, after failing at several business ventures and self-publishing an autobiography he sold door-to-door, died a pauper in the charity ward of Chicago's Cook County Hospital.

And I uncovered a biography of Charles "Mile-a-Minute"

Murphy. In 1899, he amazed the sporting world by reaching a speed of fifty-eight miles per hour on a bicycle that he raced behind a Long Island Railroad steam locomotive equipped with a special shield to cut wind resistance. Murphy ended up on the New York Police Department's bike patrol, chasing "scorchers" (speeders) who exceeded the eight-mile-an-hour limit. There was even a time at the turn of the century when British scouts used folding bicycles in the Boer War and military analysts predicted the bicycle would become an important part of future warfare. "The bicycle," said a British general in South Africa, "has proved very useful during the present war. The rider is less conspicuous than he would be on a horse, though of course he has to risk punctures and gears going out of order."

I started finding so much interesting stuff that I opened a file in my computer titled "BIKEHIST," and the larger it got, the greater my sense of mission became. Pedaling all day and making the next town by nightfall was no longer enough. I needed to fill my head with something other than thoughts of potholes and headwinds.

2

MY SENSE OF DIRECTION ESCAPES ME WHEN I TRY TO NAVI-gate a city by car. Even in familiar territory, like Washington, D.C., the confluence of streets and avenues pouring into a roundabout throws me into confusion and I invariably head off in the wrong direction, even if I have traveled the route a dozen times. "You should have gone right," my wife will say, and she is always correct. But my misturns do not fluster me because, given time, I have never failed to arrive eventually at an intended destination. The bicycle is another matter. A wrong turn could take me twenty or thirty miles out of the way, maybe even force me to retrace my steps. In a car, this might waste an hour; on a bike, a full day. So I was cautious at each fork, weighing alternatives in terms of time and miles, and only once, coming out of Chattanooga, did I misread my map. The problem was that the road didn't go where I wanted to go. The only direct route west was Interstate 24, but since I wasn't permitted to ride it, I had to follow a secondary road north for half a day before linking with one that eventually turned west. I biked for a long while, mostly uphill, and thought I was on the outskirts of Tracy City. Several hours without coffee had produced caffeine withdrawal and a headache. I needed a café. By an abandoned truck stop that, I was told, had once serviced over-the-road drivers with home-cooked meals and prostitutes, I happened on seven Tennessee state police cars blocking the two-lane country road. The patrolmen were stopping and searching cars from both directions and I pulled into line, behind a red pickup with two nasty-looking German shepherds in the cargo hold, to await my turn. "Not you," an officer said, waving me to the head of the line. "You can keep going."

"How far to the next cup of coffee?" I asked.

"That'd be Tracy City, I guess. Hey, Jess, how far'd you say it is to Tracy City?"

"Twenty-five miles, maybe thirty," Jess said.

I was stunned to have so underestimated my progress and when the road leveled out near Haletown on the Tennessee River I pulled into a general store to examine my map. In the distance I could see I-24 heading right where I wanted to go. But my only way across the river and what the locals called Nigger Jack Lake was on a narrow two-lane bridge that had charged a toll before the interstate came through. Two woodsy-looking young men were filling several quart jars at the gas pump. Their hair was long and unkempt and their remaining teeth were in bad shape. I smelled redneck trouble. Rednecks and dogs share similar views of bicyclists and I decided to keep my distance, pretending to be engrossed in my map, which unfortunately almost always leads to a conversation. They wandered over and seemed friendly enough. I asked how they spent their time in Haletown.

"Huntin' and fishin', fishin' and huntin'," one of them said. "Catchin' catfish mostly. That's all anybody does 'round here. My daddy caught the biggest catfish in the county last year, seventy-two pounds. It's in the county records and everything."

"How come you stuck around Haletown?" I said. "I thought people left small towns as soon as they got out of high school."

"Not 'round here. Where else you goin' to find huntin' and fishin' like this? No one leaves. They stay. Their parents die and they move back into the family house and add on. Me, I like the city for a visit but it scares me. Too many hassles. I wouldn't live anywhere else 'cept here."

I relaxed, and felt foolish about having been uneasy in the first place. Billy and Sparkie—adults who used first names ending in "y" or "ie" always puzzled me unless they were baseball players—wanted to know why so many people were killing one another in Washington and they told me about Haletown and catfish and they asked how I was going to get out of town. "Why, on the old toll bridge over there, I guess," I said. Sparkie took off his visored cap, gave his hair a good scratching and shook his head.

"That bridge is too narrow," he said. "Two lanes, no shoulder, no margin at all. You get two coal trucks really rolling like they do and they're passing you in different directions at the same time, you got two choices: Jump into the river, or jump up and try to hold on to one of the bridge's cables. Otherwise you just get flattened. We had an ole boy walking 'cross the bridge just last week. He mighta had a bit too much to drink and he decides he'll walk the center lane. There was two trucks passing the same time. They saw him and tried to pull over but there's no place to go. The driver's mirror hit him, pow!"—Sparkie slapped his cheek to make the point—"and took off his head. I'd hate to see that happen to you."

"Me, too."

There was a long moment of silence as we contemplated my dilemma. "What I could do," Billy said, "is block traffic for you with my truck till you're over the bridge." It was a fine idea and I pedaled onto the span, hogging the center of the right lane. Billy and Sparkie followed, two or three feet behind my rear wheel. The first few hundred yards were an ascent and I worked flat-out but could manage only 6 mph. The cars and coal trucks stacked up behind Billy's pickup. No one honked or cursed (at least not loud enough for me to hear). Midway across, the road dipped downward. The far bank in sight, I picked up speed . . . 15 mph . . . 20 . . . and reached the river's edge with little energy to spare. I pulled off onto a gravel shoulder. Billy and Sparkie tossed me a wave and two toothless smiles as they sped away, leading the now unhindered line of traffic. I hoped to find them parked up the road so I could say a proper thank-you, but when I crested the hill their pickup was nowhere in sight, and I went on, my debt to strangers growing by the day.

The land changed as I closed in on Memphis. It grew flatter and lusher. The road widened and soon I was on a wide, beautiful shoulder. The forest gave way to open fields. Dogs watched me go by but did not give chase. The headwinds subsided and I started making good time again, knocking off fourteen or fifteen miles in an hour. My bicycle felt a part of me, like skis do on an effortless downhill run. My cadence had become steady. I shifted through the range of gears without thinking, without straining. Every now and then I clicked on my odometer to see how far I had gone since the last check but mostly, however briefly, I had forgotten about miles. The fast, easy movement of my bike was elating, a sort of tranquilizer that lulled the mind into thoughtlessness and made the body feel surprisingly strong and responsive.

I had a particular reason for wanting to get to Memphis on time: Sandy was flying from Washington to join me there for the weekend. To buy the cheapest ticket, she had had to book her flight ten days before departure, when I was six hundred or so miles out of Memphis. This was no small logistical feat, trying to lay plans that would get a jet and a bicycle to the same city at the same time, but somehow it was working, and as I headed through Memphis on Danny Thomas Boulevard, paralleling the Mississippi, I was a day ahead of schedule and nearly a thousand miles from home. I used the extra time to file an article to the *Times* and call VOA. I stocked up on raisins and bananas, found a deserted Laundromat where I could strip down to my briefs and throw everything else into the washer, and bought a pint of whiskey from a shop whose owner kept the door bolted and sold his wares from behind a bulletproof window that opened onto the street.

There was an article in the local paper that said nearly half the city's eleventh graders knew someone who had been shot and one in five admitted carrying a weapon to class for protection. Truckers, fearing ambushes at red lights, told me they dodged around some of the main thoroughfares to avoid the inner city. This old cotton capital, once the most important river town between New Orleans and St. Louis, was a troubled place. It had the feel of a city that had tried and was failing. Everyone with money had moved out toward Germantown or into the communities along the Mississippi. The downtown pedestrian mall, as pleasing to the eye as it was, emptied out at dusk, save for the drifters and homeless who sat on benches, watching the trolley pass by row after row of tacky variety stores. Even Beale Street, once alive with gambling joints and hookers and the finest blues anywhere, seemed to be broken down and living on memories. When I asked where I could find a bookstore, the hotel porter said, "I don't believe you can downtown. They've all moved out to the suburbs." He ran down a list of what nearby streets were safe at night and which weren't and advised, "You'll find it best to take a cab." Having given my personal security on country roads not a thought for so long, it was annoying to be reminded that in the city I once again had to keep my defenses up.

3

I CONSIDERED RIDING TO THE AIRPORT TO MEET SANDY ON my bicycle but dismissed the idea as impractical and hotdoggish. So I rented a car. It felt peculiar to be buckled into a seat, careering along I-55 at breakneck speed, air conditioner humming, no sound of wind or passing traffic penetrating the rolled-up windows. Sandy's nonstop flight arrived on time—her trip to Memphis took two hours and forty minutes; mine, three weeks—and she bounced off the plane carrying a large stack of mail, several inner tubes and a bunch of bicycle maps detailing a new route to California, through Texas, in case snow in the Rockies forced me south. I had declined her offer to bring me new street clothes, explaining that the chinos with a rip in the knee had become a road badge of honor. "You look great, really fit," she said, which is exactly what I had hoped she would say. I had almost forgotten the joy of being with a loved one. The vicissitudes of the highway suddenly felt insignificant and my journey seemed an extraordinarily lonely affair. I was in no hurry to reclaim my life hugging the white line. Going nowhere was a lot less work. Sandy and I went aboard the *Delta Queen* paddle wheeler that had stopped in Memphis on its way up-river; we stopped by the Peabody Hotel, where five resident ducks, guided by the hotel duckmaster, waddled each morning through the ornate lobby to a fountain, and spent the day swimming, until summoned back to the elevator that returned them to their rooftop home. We visited the home of the most successful dead man alive (Elvis's Graceland brought 800,000 people a year to Memphis) and spent an afternoon at the motel (and now civil rights museum) where Martin Luther King Jr. was killed. Our stops taken as a whole—a slain civil rights leader, a pill-popping celebrity dead at age forty-two, a duckmaster, a historic paddle wheeler plying the Mississippi—seemed an oddly contradictory American experience.

Sandy left the hotel early Sunday morning to catch a plane back to Washington. Three days of comfort and companionship had weakened my resolve and, had I been prodded, I could have packed up my bike and joined her on the flight without great remorse. Heck, I could always say I had biked to Memphis, which struck me as pretty astounding. I dawdled about the hotel for a long time, drinking coffee and reading the *Commercial Appeal.* I stubbed out one cigarette and lit another. I went up to my room and back to the lobby. From the Holiday Inn Crowne Plaza's windows I could see a line of cars and eighteen-wheelers crossing the Mississippi into Arkansas on the Hernando de Soto Memorial Bridge. They were on Interstate 40, a straight, 2,000-mile shot to Barstow, California, with not so much as a traffic light to slow their pace. Their drivers would beat me there by weeks but they would know no more about America when they arrived than they had when they left.

"Okay, quit dillydallying. Time to get on with it," I said to myself, convinced that Sandy's plane really had taken off and she was not about to magically reappear in the lobby to announce that all flights to Washington had been canceled for the week. I changed into shorts and a jersey and pushed my bike down the eleventh-floor corridor and into the elevator. Heads in the lobby turned in my direction and a bellman followed me outside to ask how I managed to stay hunched over the handlebars all day without going numb. "Actually," I said, "if you keep flexing your arms and back and neck, it's pretty comfortable." I followed Second Street over to Third and turned right on Crump Boulevard, which leads onto the old Memphis Arkansas Bridge spanning the Mississippi. It was 9 A.M. and weekend traffic was light. The bridge has a narrow pedestrian walkway, protected from the travel lanes by a sturdy railing, and I chose it for my river crossing, even though its surface was littered with broken glass, chunks of driftwood, used condoms, syringes, and occasionally a discarded shoe. I rode slowly in order to dodge the obstacles. Since presumably only poor people and an occasional wayward biker—cross the river under foot power, the highway department apparently felt it could ignore any maintenance obligations. The bridge hangs low over the water and there is something both thrilling and ominous to glide by so close to the Mississippi that I could hear the gurgle of its currents. At the river's midpoint I left Tennessee and entered Arkansas.

Though I thought of each day as a collection of ten- or twelve-mile segments that I took on one at a time, the overall journey had a different dimension: If knocking off a segment was a first down, then crossing a state line was a touchdown. I planned my route from border to border, thinking of the United States not as a single continent of interminable distance but, like Europe, a group of countries, or states, in which my concern was only to get to the next one. I stopped on the Arkansas side of the bridge and removed the frayed and torn Tennessee map from the see-through plastic window on my handlebar bag. In its place went a new, crisply creased Arkansas map. Fort Smith on the Oklahoma border looked to be about eight days away.

I turned north toward Marion, the Mississippi Plain as flat as it was broad. Cotton fields reached out to the east and west. The frontage road I traveled ran alongside I-55, which, since our north–south interstates are numbered from 95 on the Atlantic to 5 on the Pacific, marked roughly a third of the way across the United States. I coasted through the farming towns of Jericho and Clarkedale, each with a little general store and a population that appeared to be all black, and cut west on Route 14, which wanders into the Ozark Mountains. The plain gave way to rolling hills, one after another, up and down, up and down, and I shifted constantly to maintain an easy pace. I passed a drive-in theater whose marquee advertised "DUble feATURe" (hadn't drive-ins gone out of business years ago?) and a drive-in restaurant with miniskirted carhops serving hamburgers and Pepsis on trays that attached to their customers' windows. Graying tufts of cotton hung from harvested bushes in the fields and along one stretch of 14 the bayou became so dense with tall, tangled vines that I pedaled harder and would not have been surprised to discover trolls peering at me through fallen limbs.

By the time I reached the town of Marked Tree, forty miles out of Memphis, it was nearly 1 P.M. Sandy, I figured, had already covered a thousand miles and been home for an hour or two. I found a restaurant just off the main street and ordered a cheeseburger, two milk shakes and a side of onion rings. A black-and-white TV at the end of the counter chattered on, its volume rising and falling as bolts of fuzziness blurred the picture. There was only one other customer in the place, an overweight teenage girl who sat two tables over.

"Well, what do you think about Haiti?" she asked the elderly proprietress.

" 'Bout what?" the older woman replied, looking up from the grill where my cheeseburger sizzled.

"Haiti. Clinton's flying three dudes down there to talk and it looks like we're going to make peace, not war. We've still got troops going in, though. What're we doing flying B-52s down there, full of food and money and heaven knows what else? All the problems right here at home, that's what we ought to be paying attention to. Haiti's their country. Let them do with it what they want, wouldn't you say?"

"Oh, I don't know. I haven't paid it no mind."

Although I'd put in nearly enough miles to qualify for a full day's work, it was too early to quit. I spread the Arkansas map over my table. The next town to the west that looked large enough to have a motel was Newport. It was fifty-six miles away, more than I could handle by nightfall, and I wondered why, when traveling by car, towns always seemed spaced just about right where you wanted them to be. On a bicycle they were either ten miles too close or ten miles too distant. I asked the girl if she knew what the next town with a motel was. She looked at me as though I'd asked her to explain the theory of relativity. "Oh, Lord," she said, "I wouldn't know *that*." Every now and then the lack of curiosity I encountered startled me. Only here and now mattered. The next town over might as well be another planet and if a topic hadn't been on *Oprah,* it probably wasn't worth wasting much time discussing. We all had access to enough news and information to drown in, yet pockets of America remained as intellectually isolated as nineteenth-century outposts on the Western frontier. There was only one way to answer the question the girl could not: I pedaled west.

4

We hear no more of the clangin' hoof,
And the stage-coach rattling by . . .
And the old pike road is left alone
And the stagers seek the plow;
We have circled the earth with an iron rail,
And the steam-king rules us now.

—Rev. John Pierpont

In 1916 the united states had the world's largest rail network, over 250,000 miles of track that crisscrossed the cities and reached out to the most distant hamlets. Steam had indeed taken command of the nation's transportation corridors but that year, with two million cars registered in the United States, President Wilson signed legislation recognizing the growing popularity—and future dominance—of the automobile. The Federal Aid Road Act appropriated $75 million for highway improvements, theoretically to speed mail over "post roads." The first beneficiary was a 2½-mile stretch of highway in California, from the Alameda County border to the Richmond Road near San Francisco. In those days, with most roads unmarked, conditions primitive, the transcontinental Lincoln Highway still in its early planning stages and road maps both rare and unreliable beyond the county level, motorists on journeys of any distance traveled as bicyclists do today: They went from town to town; they asked directions of farmers along the way; they charted their trip carefully to take into account the likelihood of finding gas stations, repair facilities, hotels and food. Motoring was guess-work. As the Hartford Rubber Works tire company noted in its *Automobile Good Roads and Tours,* published in the 1910s: "A very thorough preliminary search showed that there were no maps which could be used as a basis for this work. . . . Much has been willingly left to geographical sense, and the tourist's own constructive faculty."

What passed for maps at the dawn of the automobile era were actually guides with text, published by various companies in bound or folded form, that helped motorists navigate from landmark to landmark, the landmarks often being trees or barns or cafés. The 1916 edition of the *Automobile Blue Standard Road Guide of America* took two full pages to detail the eighty-two-mile trip from Hartford, Connecticut, to Worcester, Massachusetts: ". . . From city hall 0.3 miles and bear left with the trolley on Connecticut Blvd. and 32.1 miles to West Stafford, at 3-corners with wood church on left, straight thru on macadam and across state line in Mass at 46.3; stone water-trough in fork, keep right . . ." (The guides were designed for whites; African-Americans used the *Negro Motorist Green Book,* published from 1936 to 1963, which listed cabins and out-of-the-way restaurants where they were welcome.) Rand McNally's popular Photo-Auto Guides contained a picture of every corner or point where the road changed directions on selected routes. It wasn't until 1922, when the last of the nation's stagecoaches were disappearing from their few remaining scheduled runs in the West, that Rand McNally published its first complete set of U.S. state road maps for motorists, and not until 1926 did oil companies conceive the idea of giving free maps to drivers who purchased their gasoline.

In many ways planning my own trip was reminiscent of the uncertainties the early motorists faced. Should I cross the country from east to west and buck the prevailing winds, or from west to east, which would mean enduring the Mojave when desert temperatures were dangerously high? Should I follow the mountainous northern route from Seattle to Bar Harbor, Maine—the most scenic way and, at 4,415 miles, the longest—or the southernmost route from San Diego to St. Augustine, Florida, which is a thousand miles shorter, tediously flat and, at my pace, includes about two weeks in Texas looking at nothing? Or how about just getting on Route 20 in Boston—the longest two-lane road in the United States—and following it the 3,200 miles to Newport, Oregon? Should I leave in spring when I'm going to encounter a lot of rain but no snow, or summer when there's crippling heat but no cold, or autumn when it's dry but sometimes prematurely wintery in pockets of the Mountain West? I studied maps, examined Greyhound schedules, consulted others who had crossed the country by bicycle. Every time I made a firm decision, someone would say, "But have you considered . . . ?" and, admitting I hadn't, I'd start plotting a new route. Finally someone suggested I get in touch with Bikecentennial in Missoula, Montana.

Bikecentennial—now named Adventure Cycling—goes back, in concept anyway, to 1972, when no one but an occasional eccentric rode a bicycle cross-country and there wasn't any such thing as a transcontinental "route slip," which is what cyclists call bike maps. Two couples—Greg and June Siple and Dan and Lys Burden—set off that year to bicycle the eighteen thousand miles from Alaska to Argentina, and somewhere en route, no doubt desperate for something, *anything*, new to talk about to break the tedium, they came up with the idea of organizing a mass cross-country bike ride to celebrate the nation's bicentennial. Once back in Montana, they plotted out the TransAmerica Bicycle Trail, a forty-two-hundred-mile back-road route that starts in Astoria, Oregon, dips down through Yellowstone National Park to Pueblo, Colorado, then turns due east to Yorktown, Virginia. Two thousand cyclists went coast-to-coast on it in 1976. The age of bicycle touring had arrived. In the years since the bicentennial, Adventure Cycling, a nonprofit organization that promotes the bicycle as a means of discovery and adventure, has mapped a National Bicycle Route Network, encompassing twenty thousand miles of roads up and down and across North America. I sent off for a stack of its maps and was struck that, in scope and detail, they bore great resemblance to the *Blue Standard Road Guides* motorists had used eighty years earlier. They tell you where you can get your bike repaired and find food, motels, hostels and campgrounds, what the elevation, weather and road conditions are. In reading how to navigate Virginia's Henrico County, I might as well have been studying a road guide from the 1920s: "Turn right on CR [county road] 663 then bend left paralleling the railroad. 17 miles to Ashland. Turn left on Center St. . . . Turn left on Patrick St. In .25 miles turn on Taylor Rd. which becomes CR 667."

There's nothing wrong, of course, with just getting a bunch of state maps and heading out on an unplanned route, improvising as you go. But as much as I liked to kid myself into believing I traveled on a whim, I wanted the security of knowing where I was going and how I would get there. Though I realized that biking west to east, and thus toward, rather than away from, home, would offer psychological support, I decided to dismiss the significance of mind games and the prevailing winds and go east to west. That would put me in the Mojave in October or November, when temperatures were manageable and would reinforce my notion that the romance of America's roads has always flowed in a westerly direction. Los Angeles, my former home, became the destination for no other reason than the old Route 66 had ended there, at the Santa Monica Pier, and when I had first seen California as a teenager, having hitchhiked across the country and followed 66 a good portion of the way, that is where, nearly forty years earlier, my journey had ended, too.

Adventure Cycling hadn't developed a route slip that starts or ends in Los Angeles, because, its people told me, most bikers want to avoid the desert. So in the end I put myself in the hands of Norty Stewart. It was his orange line that had been drawn across my fourteen maps. Stewart had spent a career with AAA in Southern California as a travel consultant, planning trips for motorists, when a man walked into his office one day, many years ago, and asked him to map a bicycle route to Ventura, fifty miles away. "I looked at him and

thought, well, here's one out of the kooky ward," Stewart re-
called. "I was quite taken aback." But the popularity of bicycle touring was growing and word spread. Before long
Stewart was receiving requests from people around the world
and throughout the country who wanted to discover the
United States by bicycle. He became the guru of odd cross-
ings. He mapped routes for hundreds of cyclists and a group
of horsemen who wanted to ride from Boston's Old North
Church to Newport Beach, California, to celebrate the two
hundredth anniversary of the signing of the Bill of Rights. He
planned coast-to-coast routes for walkers, joggers, roller
skaters and a boy on crutches, and though not much of a biker
himself after suffering two strokes, he came to know every
pothole between Los Angeles and New York, which way the
winds blow in the Texas Panhandle, when the first snows are
likely to fall in Colorado, what sections of Route 66 are still
bikeable and whether Farmington, New Mexico, or Flagstaff,
Arizona, has better repair facilities. "I found it a lot more
challenging than trying to get someone from A to B in his
car," Stewart said. Triple-A received good PR from Stewart's
efforts, but the company wasn't in business to service bicyclists, and on a somewhat unpleasant note, Stewart took early
retirement at the age of sixty-one and set up Singing Wheels
Touring in the bedroom of his Glendale, California, apartment, which he shares with shelf upon shelf of bicycle books
and enough state, city, and county maps to give Rand
McNally a run for its money. I reached Stewart on the phone
in his bedroom and he grilled me abut my preferences—
mountains or flatlands, motels or campgrounds, thoroughfares or secondary roads?—and in exchange for thirty dollars
Express Mailed me the fourteen personalized maps that had

now gotten me to Marked Tree, Arkansas. The eleventh one in the series covered a segment of northern Arizona and was titled "Indian Country." It sounded too remote to contemplate. I put it at the bottom of the stack and tried to forget about Arizona entirely.

5

I RACED THE APPROACHING NIGHT TO NEWPORT. STORM clouds were rolling in from my rear, filling the Arkansas countryside with dark, long shadows, but they did not gain on me and I figured the front and I were traveling at about the same speed, ten or twelve miles an hour. If I could maintain my pace for the next few hours, I could make Newport by nightfall. On my rear rack, I carried a one-pound sleeping bag, hardly larger than a loaf of bread, wrapped in plastic: I considered it only an emergency backup and hoped I'd be able to make California without ever unwrapping it. I associate camping out not with great wilderness experiences but with being in places I didn't really want to be—a hilltop firebase in Vietnam during the war, a refugee camp in Tanzania during the Rwanda massacres, a Somali guerrilla outpost during the now forgotten Ogaden war against Ethiopia. Despite my fear of biking at night, I was prepared to ride halfway around the clock to avoid pitching camp along some untraveled highway. This was a different kind of apprehension than

I knew in the city, where a sense of evil often prowls the night and dark, deserted streets can feel as spooky as anything I know. Here, in the Ozark foothills, I had no fear of my environment. My apprehension dwelled entirely in a single concern—the possible denial of creature comforts. A clean bed, a warm shower, access to an ice machine and food of even marginal quality was the reward the highway offered in exchange for a day's work. Enduring primitive conditions when schlepping through the Third World in pursuit of wars and coups d'état was part of the excitement and challenge of newspapering, but on a voluntary mission, I'd aim for a margin of comfort every time. I checked my watch. It was 5:30 P.M. Newport was still twenty-four miles off.

For the first time on the trip, I turned on my lights, in Amagon. The town had been all but abandoned. The Texaco station was now a pool hall and all ten stores on the main street had been boarded up. Towns, like people, are born, evolve, die, yet there is something unnatural about a ghost town, because its presence is a mark of shared failure. Did the former inhabitants take their dreams with them or just give up and move on? Who was the first to go and why did the occupants of the last half dozen homes huddled beyond the pool hall stay? Why does one town die while another up the road lives on? I leaned my bike against a tree, ignoring the need to make time, and had a smoke on the curb. My three water bottles were nearly empty and I decided to conserve what was left until my thirst grew greater. I would have liked to have had someone to talk to but no one was around. "What happened to Amagon?" I asked, and a voice in me answered back, "Hadn't you heard? The crops failed a while back after three summers of drought. The Joneses left, then the Edwardses and Washingtons. Mr. Caswell, who ran the hardware store, moved to Batesville and you remember Sam, the barber; he died a couple of winters back. His children got to fighting over the place—what was worth fighting over, I don't know—and the last I heard they were down by Conway, or maybe it was Morrilton. They just walked away. You'll still find Everett Brown walking the road with his dog every night at dusk, like he's been doing for long as I can remember. That's about all that's still the same. Fact is Everett asked just the other day if I thought you'd ever come back to Amagon. . . ." It was just as well no one was around to hear me carrying on a conversation of make-believe history. I found myself doing this quite often but did not take it as a sign of going daffy. I mounted up. Route 14 disappeared into a curtain of darkness ahead. At the edge of town, I could make out the form of someone walking in a half-shuffle toward me. A raggedy collie padded along at his heel. The man was old and stoop shouldered and I passed too quickly to make out his face. I heard him say, "Evenin'," and, startled by his presence, I had no chance to reply. I started to brake fifty yards down the road, with the thought of turning back to talk and ask his name, but when I glanced over my shoulder, I could no longer see the old man or his dog, so I continued on my way.

My lights afforded little protection or visibility. The pulsating red light attached to my sleeping bag would probably catch the eye of an approaching driver at fifty yards, though the battery-operated one on the handlebar wasn't much stronger than the toy light I had on my old Schwinn when I was a kid. It cast a flickering glow on the road a few feet ahead and left me mostly in darkness. The miles passed slowly and the night turned cold. Around me the landscape—hills and trees, an occasional barn, a long fence rambling along the road's shoulder—appeared flat and one-dimensional, like charcoal lines on an artist's canvas. Only three cars passed in an hour's time. Finally, just before nine o'clock, I saw the lights of a town in the valley ahead. A sign said, NEWPORT 7. Farther down the road the next sign said, NEWPORT 9. I took no pleasure in tricks played so late in the day. The Lake Side Inn in Newport is on Madison Street, and although there is no lake and motels that call themselves inns are always suspect, the neon VACANCY sign was a welcome invitation. I had covered ninety-six miles since breakfast in Memphis. The town's fast-food restaurants were closed, and in my room, I reached into my saddlebag for dinner, withdrawing a vanilla crunch Crypto Bar that the label advertised as "performance nutrition." It tasted like hay, and, at $1.50, probably wasn't any more nourishing than a 25-cent box of raisins. A glass of whiskey made me light-headed. I decided the day was over. Before going to bed I made a note of the typewritten message taped to the bathroom mirror: WARNING! TOWELS ARE INVENTORIED IMMEDIATELY AFTER CHECKOUT. CLOTHS FOR REMOVING GREASE ARE AVAILABLE IN THE OFFICE.

If nothing else, I had become a champion sleeper on the journey. I went to bed early, often at nine-thirty or ten o'clock, not because I was exhausted but because there was seldom anything else to do once the laundry was washed, the journal updated, the bike checked over, the map studied, the meal eaten. Unless a particularly hard day lay ahead, I established no precise time for my morning departures and simply headed out whenever I awoke and was ready to go. It was a life of abandon and one that no doubt had ruined me for future employment where obedient wage earners are expected to live by a schedule. I felt no guilt when I set off late, felt no guilt that I was no longer bringing home a weekly paycheck, felt no guilt to have lost myself on the highways far from home. The sense of outrunning guilt and responsibility was exhilarating.

There was the damnedest sight when I left the Lake Side the next morning. Eight or nine guests were in the parking lot, wiping down their pickups with rags. Several had the hoods up and were cleaning their engines. One man had crawled under his vehicle and was working on something or other with a wrench. It was as though I had stumbled into a flea market for truck lovers. I mentioned how odd this looked to the young girl who checked me out and inventoried my towels and she pointed to a shiny red pickup with oversized wheels and said, "If I had a rig like that, I'd keep it clean too." I was beginning to like Arkansas. It was shamelessly unpretentious and when people referred to me in the plural with, "Now, y'all come back," I had the feeling they meant it. No one gave a hoot how many grams of fat were in a blueberry muffin, and all the topics earnestly discussed at dinner parties in Washington—the President's popularity rating, what Congress was up to, who the Republicans would choose as a candidate for the White House—didn't rate two sentences in rural Arkansas. Here the talk was of weather, crops and high school football. The gap between rural and urban America seemed very wide, like neighboring countries that shared a common language but spoke of things that were not of mutual concern. For a city slicker I felt strangely comfortable in this new setting and I remembered what Ma Joad had said in Steinbeck's *Grapes of Wrath* about people who lived in out-of-the-way places like the ones that were now my temporary home: "I'm learnin' one thing good. Learnin' it all the time, ever' day. If you're in trouble or hurt or need, go to poor people. They're the only one's that'll help, the only ones."

Route 14 carried me across the Ozark Plateau, through Macks, Oil Trough, Rosie, Salado, Locust Grove and St. James. Rice was being harvested in the fields and the tractors stirred up swarms of mosquitoes that pattered against my helmet like raindrops. The storm clouds that had followed me into Newport had slipped away, replaced by a clear, bright autumn morning. The road was good and by the time I stopped for coffee and first checked my odometer, I had already eaten up twenty miles.

6

I ALWAYS THOUGHT GAS STATIONS WERE PLACES WHERE YOU got fuel and not much else. That's how it is at home, anyway. But in the America where I now traveled gas stations are replacing the general store and café as the commercial anchor of the community; in the process they have become the equivalent of nineteenth-century stagecoach stops. As often as not in Tennessee and Arkansas, if I wanted to buy groceries, send a fax, get a newspaper, sit at a table for coffee and a sandwich, make a phone call or peruse a deli, I had one choice—the local gas station. It was not a pleasing sign of progress, because each was the image of the other and all had been stripped of the character that permeates a good café where locals gather for coffee and idle chatter. Still, I made do; when I was sufficiently thirsty, hungry, weary or in need of talk, a gas station squatting along some barren stretch of highway could offer an agreeable reprieve. And I was looking for a reprieve as I closed in on Mountain View. The hills had been troublesome all day, forcing me into my granny gear a good part of the way. So much sweat had fallen from my brow onto the top tube of the bike frame that the shiny green bar had lost its luster. I passed a farmhouse set a hundred yards back from the road. Two youngish men with beards sat on the porch steps, holding beer bottles, and as I went by one of them yelled out, "Don't get that fucking thing on my property!" What the hell did he think—that I was going to veer off the road and ride across his crappy lawn? I started to flash them the bird but thought better of it. Two to one is lousy odds when you're alone. Besides, yahoos, not understanding they are yahoos, are beyond redemption and I didn't want to give them the satisfaction of knowing I had heard the remark by even turning my head.

Though I could count the number of dolts I had encountered since leaving home on the fingers of one hand, I was mystified as to why the sight of an adult bicyclist raises the hackles of so many motorists and people of limited mental capacity. Back in Virginia one dimwit had tossed a beer bottle at me from his pickup, and a friend who used to commute to work by bicycle in Fairbanks, Alaska, told me how passing drivers delighted in heaving bottles that smashed on the pavement just ahead of his tires, making flats unavoidable. Every biker has similar stories and they all involve beer bottles and pickups. At first I thought we are targets merely because we share the road and cause delays. Then I thought it was because we look funny in our tight shorts and multicolored jerseys and pointed shoes. Or because we are a symbol of frivolous idleness astride what is viewed as a child's plaything. In the end, the answer, I decided, was simple: Alone on the road, we are defenseless, and the drivers who hurl bottles and take pleasure in giving us fright with high-speed, close-in passes are the grown-up version of the bullies we remember from school who only picked on kids too weak to fight back. I've never heard of a biker being taunted by just one man in a car; it always takes two.

Actually, knowing I would be traveling in places where odd clothing was looked upon as less than manly, I was anxious not to call attention to myself and had gone to lengths to avoid biking attire that appeared too flaky or stylish. The Performance catalog where I did my shopping in preparation for the trip was full of fancy gear: bib tights, toe booties, Lycra shorts ablaze in reds and yellows, skintight pants that gave prominence to every muscle and organ. You could spend a fortune and not even get out of your garage. My first thought was to bike, as I guess I did when I was a kid, in jeans and a T-shirt and sneakers, because what worked forty years ago usually works just fine today. But a few test runs proved this unreasonable. The jeans chafed and made my legs feel encumbered. T-shirts became sweat-drenched and clung like wet towels. The sneakers never really got a grip in the pedal toe clips. Reluctantly I came to accept that the new biking accessories, rather than being a marketing gimmick to fleece people who considered being chic a form of godliness, really did make biking easier and more comfortable. So I took the plunge, spending two hundred dollars on what the catalog listed as "Essential Cycling Equipment!" I opted for the most conservative stuff I could find: brown shorts (with padded insert liner for butt protection) that hung loose and didn't look much different than what you'd wear cutting the grass on a Saturday morning; a blue jersey (with three pockets on the backside for carrying water bottles and bananas) that had no more flash than an Arrow shirt; shoes (with cleated soles designed to clutch the pedal) that were as comfortable for walking as for biking and a lot less flamboyant than a pair of Air Jordan sneakers. Then there were socks to buy and gloves and a "cycling computer" that kept track of miles and speed and a lightweight windbreaker and a tool kit and a helmet and steel-beaded touring tires and saddlebags and little pouches that clipped onto the backside of the saddle and various tubes on the frame. The UPS man brought a new package almost daily and by the time I had finished, the bill for bringing myself and my bike up to standards had reached eight hundred dollars. At least I *looked* good, even if I didn't exactly know what I was doing. The transformation, Sandy said, was startling for an out-of-vogue tightwad who still drives a 1970 Buick, skis in a baggy blue parka bought thirty years ago and clings to a collection of neckties as wide as bibs that, no doubt, one day will be back in fashion. Clearly I had succumbed to the psyche of the 1990s.

As gas stations go, the one outside St. James wasn't bad. I fastened my bike to a *USA Today* vending machine and walked through the small parking lot that, like the entire countryside, was covered with a snowlike dusting of feathers from the multitude of nearby chicken coops. I ordered coffee, two hot dogs and a milk shake and spread out my map on the table. Even when I knew where I was going—and Route 14 was the only way into or out of St. James—I never tired of studying the flow of roads, looking for better routes, tracking numbered highways with my finger to discover where they began and ended. The routes marked in red were wider, faster and more heavily traveled, the ones in black—like 14, which led to the towns of Fifty-Six, Big Flat, Harriet and Evening Star—narrower, lonelier, more rural and unpredictable. Sometimes I found a shortcut that saved a few miles or a road that went around a mountain instead of over it, but mostly I found that Norty Stewart's orange line was carrying me on the truest passage west. "How much weight are you carrying in the panniers?" the man at the next table asked. It was a dead giveaway: He was a cyclist or he would have said *saddlebags,* not *panniers.* Uninvited, I joined him.

Bob Freeman, a charter member of the Arkansas Bicycle Club, was out for a drive in his RV. He asked me if I had had many hassles with motorists—a subject of frequent discussion when bikers recount their travels. I listed a few and he said he had giving up biking on Saturdays. The reason: His favorite route went past a beer hall near Jonesboro and he had had to dodge so many airborne bottles over the years that weekend riding was no longer fun. "I don't know why," he said, "but a lot of people just don't like cyclists." The hostility, I mentioned, went back more than a hundred years and was one of the reasons early cyclists in Europe and the United States banded together into clubs such as his. There was even a time in England, late in the nineteenth century, when restaurant and tea-shop owners refused to serve cyclists.

Describing the attitude toward "wheelmen" in America during the 1890s, Eugene Sloane writes, in *The Complete Book of Bicycling:*

> *The general populace resented cyclists, just as many people were against the early automobile. Farmers took personal delight in blocking the narrow roads of the day with the wagon,*

and they went as slowly as possible just to aggravate cyclists be-hind them. Country bumpkins took great delight in thrusting sticks between the spokes of cyclists' wheels to knock them off their seats. When people were riding the "penny-farthing" in the early days of cycling, a stick between the spokes of the high wheel brought disaster to the cyclists and guffaws from pranksters. One of the reasons the early cycling clubs were formed, aside from social purposes, was to provide protection against wanton attacks on cyclists. Horse-drawn vehicles, in ad-dition to blocking the roads, were often deliberately sent careen-ing into groups of cyclists, which injured the riders as well as harmed their machines.

In that context, the harassment I encountered seemed lit-tle more than a minor annoyance. But it made me cautious and I looked on every passing pickup as a potential enemy, though few were.

7

MY LIFE'S WORK HAS BEEN AS A REPORTER. I DON'T REMEM-ber ever wanting any other job, and it's the only job I really know how to do. I ask questions, take notes, try to explain what I have seen and heard in a coherent fashion on a piece of paper. A simple enough process. Though polls indicate that people like me command scant public respect or trust, I still hold to the belief that newspapering is among the most honorable of professions—a profession that to an extraordinary degree remains untainted by greed, scandal or personal ambitions. The best of the reporters understand they are but foot soldiers in the hierarchy of opinion-shapers. They know the impact of what they write (on issues admittedly weightier than bicycling across America) usually ranges from minimal to nonexistent; their mission is simply to get it right so others can determine the course of events. I mention this for two reasons: first, because as I have grown older I have found it difficult to separate me-the-person from me the reporter (too often I find myself conducting an interview when I should be having a conversation); and second, because the journey was not evolving as I had expected, and as a result, I had become a sort of passive reporter, listening without asking questions designed to elicit a response, seeking exchanges in brief road encounters in which both the subject and I remained strangers to each other. Unlike covering, say, the massacres in Rwanda or the Persian Gulf War in Kuwait, I had no involvement in the lives of those whose world I had entered. Rather than removing myself from the scene, as is a reporter's custom, I was now the protagonist of my own little drama. It was a role I was quite unused to.

When I set off I envisioned straying often from my route, spending a day or two here and there to explore my surroundings. I packed a camera and notebooks. But I was twelve hundred miles from home and I had yet to remove the camera from its case. I hadn't scribbled notes in public or volunteered that I worked for the *Los Angeles Times* or asked anyone his age or how to spell his name. I hadn't even done much roaming, for every unplanned mile made California more distant and the mile that captivated my thoughts was the final one onto the Santa Monica Pier. The uneasiness I first felt with my new role soon slipped away. The mind, I found, can hold images as precisely as a camera and I liked talking to people without the distraction of taking notes. It wasn't that I had stopped being a reporter; I had just learned a new way of reporting. When introductions were necessary, no longer did I mention my company affiliation in the same breath with my name. No longer did I drop into conversations references to exotic places—as, being a short learner, I discover I have just done in the previous paragraph—to prove I had been around. My identity on the road came from where I was going or how I was getting there, not from what I did for a living. Take away the bicycle and I would have been just another faceless traveler going west.

The people I met didn't much care what I did anyway. Almost none asked. They'd want to know where I was from or what my wife thought about all this nonsense but I never had the feeling they were sizing me up to determine if I were rich or poor, a conservative or a liberal, a Protestant or a Jew. Perhaps, as products of the homogeneity of thought and lifestyle that small towns breed, they just assumed anyone with whom they could share a comfortable conversation was a lot like themselves. More likely, though, was that I found in country people a vague tolerance I was not used to in the city. As long as you didn't appear different, as long as you didn't seem to stick your head above the crowd, you were accepted on face value and your station in life bore little relationship to your perceived worth. I promised myself I would never again respond to an introduction at a social occasion with something like "Nice to meet you, Bob. What do you do?"

I took State Route 66 out of Mountain View, through Newnata, Timbo, Alco and Oxley, each of which was identified on my map with a tiny circle on a black ribbon of roadway. They were empty little places, hardly more than outposts on a yet-to-be-settled frontier. I hadn't seen a billboard in days, and for countless miles not a smashed beer bottle had obstructed my way—one of the benefits, I suppose, of a dry county. The road unfolded before me like waves in a rough sea, one crest coming on top of the other, none insurmountable. As far as I could tell, not an inch of Arkansas was flat. But by shifting gears in anticipation of a hill, I was able to maintain cadence and momentum and hump my way up even the steepest grades without excessive cursing or gasping With twenty-one gears, I usually found one that felt comfortable, though I never could fathom proper shifting techniques involving gear ratios expressed in "gear inches" and mysterious combinations of gear ranges that cyclists carry as cheat sheets attached to their handlebars. All I understood was that I wasn't meant to shift sequentially, as one does in a car, from the first to the twenty first gear, and that the whole process was roughly akin to what a truck driver does when he "splits" gears to get the most efficiency from his engine. Since I was the engine, getting the most power for the least expenditure of energy was a matter of serious concern.

Coming out of Oxley, I caught the downhill side of a wave and rode it into Leslie, racing along the final mile without so much as a pedal stroke. My spirits soared and all tiredness left me when I caught a run like that. The whoosh of wind, body crouched, bike in firm control—the elation was that of barreling down a snow-covered mountain, skis perfectly parallel, the world a blur of fast-passing shadows.

Leslie sat in a trough between hills. I stopped at a corner grocery story on the main street to replenish my supply of candy bars, which I now stocked in the handlebar bag, having given up the foul-tasting nutrition bars. Two elderly men in overalls were on a bench outside the store, not talking, looking straight ahead onto the empty street. "Good afternoon," I said. They nodded. I walked my bike past them to fasten it to a light pole; then, realizing that was quite unnecessary, and maybe even offensive to the gentlemen, I left it leaning against the pole, unlocked and unattended. As I walked into the store, I saw them craning their necks to get a better look at me. The M&M's rushed right to my brain with a jolt of energy. I nodded at the two men as I retrieved my bike. "Good afternoon," one of them said.

Leslie's commercial district extended a full four blocks, giving the town an appearance of substance I had not seen in Arkansas. Back before World War II, when the Missouri and Northern Arkansas Railroad had a freight depot in Leslie, the town boomed, with a population of ten thousand. Merchants lived above their shops, in wood-frame buildings with second-floor porches that extended over the sidewalks like awnings. Farm women dressed up when they came to town Saturday mornings to do their shopping. Then the railroad pulled out of Leslie. Interstate 40 was built thirty-eight miles away—too far to funnel any business into town—and things got quiet. One after the other the merchants boarded up their shops. The bank failed, its building taken over by a coffee shop that used the vault as a walk-in ice cooler. Across the street from the old bank, an abandoned storefront was turned into Eva's Designs and a secondhand bookstore. I had not seen a bookstore—let alone anyone carrying, reading or talking about a book—since Memphis and I approached eagerly, wondering what kind of dreamer thought he could survive selling books in Leslie, Arkansas. It was Tuesday and a sign in the window said, CLOSED MON THRU WED. Nearby a hand-written note taped to the glass advised, BUSINESS FOR SALE. INQUIRE INSIDE. I tried the door but it was locked. I asked the waitress in the coffee shop, just before its daily 3 P.M. closing, what she knew about Leslie's history and she replied, "Not much. I've only lived here two years." She said Leslie had recently converted an abandoned school a few blocks away into a town museum and surely I could find all the history I wanted there.

The museum had been built largely with local funds and volunteer labor and was well appointed with thoughtful displays of Leslie's railroading and farming history. The curator seemed surprised to find anyone poking around and suggested I visit the back room that had been turned into an art gallery honoring a lifelong Leslie cartoonist who had died not long ago in his sixty-ninth year of marriage. The pen-and-ink cartoons depicted mayors and farmers and school boards and county commissioners. "It's not Rembrandt," the curator said, "but if you lived here you'd recognize the people he was drawing and the issues he was talking about." It was remarkable, I thought, that a town whose population had fallen to four hundred had put so much effort into remembering its past. Others apparently agreed too, and on a paper doily someone had put in the guest register I noted the comment: "I live in Batesville, a much larger town, and we don't have anything this nice. Congratulations on saving your history."

8

FRIENDS TOLD ME EARLY ON THAT THE JOURNEY'S MIDDLE third—roughly from Memphis to Albuquerque—would be the toughest. The newness of the experience would sustain me at the beginning, the scent of the destination at the end, but in the middle, I would fall into a sort of vacuum in which everything seemed far away and nothing felt familiar, except the routine of pedaling. They were right. The road rolled on and on and on as if I were confronting a giant treadmill, in motion but going nowhere. At times boredom overcame me and I cast an envious eye at motorists who whizzed by, radios on, knowing they could maintain a steady 60 mph no matter what the conditions of the road. Had they stopped to offer a lift, I might well have accepted. The scenery lost its texture in these moments, towns looked alike, the tedium and physical repetitiveness made it difficult to concentrate on anything except how long each mile seemed. Hadn't I been here yesterday? I'd click on my odometer, expecting to see that I'd covered ten miles or so since the last check and find I'd only ridden two or three. Boredom is the curse of an idle mind and to defeat it, I'd tell myself stories and replay old movies—John Wayne's last, *The Shootist,* wore particularly well—and remember days at the Beta House on the University of Maine campus that made me laugh. Another antidote was to take a nap. I'd lug my bike off the road and stretch out under a tree, using my helmet as a pillow. Fortunately ennui never lingered long. A good downhill run, like the one into Leslie, or an unexpected conversation over coffee or a change in the landscape—that's all it usually took to kick my head back into gear and restore my spirits.

To keep things in perspective, some evenings I'd go through notes I'd written about what others had experienced on solo bike journeys far more nervy than mine. One section I kept coming back to was about Frank Lenz, who, as a twenty-five-year-old writer for *Outing* magazine, had taken off on a "safety" bicycle in 1892 to follow the course of the sun around the world. He rode the 4,857 miles from New York City to San Francisco in 107 days and boarded the U.S.S. *Oceanic* to Yokohama. "To wheel around the world is no trifling task," he wrote before leaving the United States, "and I began to realize the magnitude of my undertaking when I was about to pass beyond the confines of my native continent. . . . Sometimes I vaguely wondered what might await me in lands oversea, and was I to face any serious perils." He pedaled across Japan, where villagers greeted him warmly, but in Shanghai was warned by the American consul-general that it was impossible to get through China's interior on a bicycle. He took off anyway, following the telegraph lines 3,000 miles inland. The Chinese were hostile, the winter was severe, and to get over mountains, he had to hire coolies to carry his bicycle and gear, which weighed 145 pounds, including a cumbersome photographic outfit. Roads were few and in one stretch of 539 miles he was able to ride only 34. He finally crossed the border into Burma, took a ship to Calcutta, and biked through what is now Pakistan to reach Persia, then Turkey. Before heading for Erzurum, the capital of Turkish Armenia, where banditry and lawlessness were rampant, he wrote: "[Thinking of] America, which I left just two years ago, I must confess to a feeling of homesickness. I am tired, very tired, of being a 'stranger.' I long for the day which will see me again on my native hearthstone and my wanderings at an end." The dispatch, written April 27, 1894, reached his New York office five weeks later. No other communications followed, and after two months his editors at *Outing* commissioned an extensive search. It yielded no clues, and no traces of his body were ever found. Lordy. And I complained when the road had no shoulder.

I did not share the feeling of homesickness of which Lenz wrote—I had, after all, in the broad sense, never left "home"—but I understood the lonely echo of his words. However you travel, however aimless your route, the open road allows you, as no other place, to lose yourself with a sense of purpose. It can swallow you up, make you feel small, abandon you in nowhere P.O. towns. Yet it can also sustain you with its sense of expectation, of new beginnings and dreamed-of destinations.

My evening long-distance calls to friends were more frequent now. So were the postcards I mailed, carrying updates on my progress. "Closing in on Oklahoma border," I wrote from Marshall, Arkansas, to a friend. "No mishaps. No rain. A few flats. All in all, I feel like a million bucks." I called the *Times* in Los Angeles and asked for Mike Kennedy, who had biked coast-to-coast after graduating from college, many years earlier, and planned to join me in Nevada for the last leg to Santa Monica. I told him I could do with a few less mountains and a lot more "wet" counties.

"By the time you get through Oklahoma, the worst will be over," he said.

"You mean the mountains?" I asked hopefully.

"No, the dry counties."

The road from Marshall to Harrison—Route 65—was crowded with charter buses carrying elderly couples from half a dozen Southern states to Branson, Missouri, thirty-five miles north. Branson, once one of the P.O. towns, had reinvented itself with wall-to-wall theaters offering family-style entertainment that had a ring of the fifties: the Lennon Sisters, Donny and Marie, Johnny Cash, Wayne Newton. Its booming prosperity had saved not only Branson but a string of way-station service towns in Arkansas. "These old people just love it," said Robert Rideaux, who had carried a full load of charter passengers from New Orleans, via an overnight motel stop in Little Rock. We sat at a rear table in a hillside shop that sold meals and Ozark handicrafts, sharing a thermos of coffee, while his passengers wolfed down a buffet breakfast. "They get into Branson, they wander from show to show. The food's good, and cheap. The entertainment's wholesome, something you'd not be embarrassed to take your kids to. There's no crime. It's just a lot of fun and you can have fun without worrying about all the things you worry about in the city." We drank three cups each in thirty minutes, then Rideaux went table to table, saying, "Time to finish up, folks. Next stop Branson." He snubbed out his cigarette and stood by the door of his bus as the passengers boarded, greeting each with a pleasantry. "Aren't you a sweetheart!" a blue-haired lady said. I watched Rideaux back into a turnaround at the side of the restaurant and head north on 65, and I remember thinking how fragile and insignificant my bicycle had looked parked next to his big, silvery coach.

I wasn't quite ready to start moving again. I went back inside and browsed through some local cookbooks—catfish and beans appeared to be staples—and started talking to the young waitress who had served us coffee. She said she was "a songwriter and performer" and had moved here from Colorado to be near Branson, where she hoped her new career would begin.

"I heard you tell the driver you're from Washington," she said, then added a bit accusingly, "You're not with the government, are you?"

"Actually," I said, "I'm from just outside Washington. But, no, I'm not with the government."

"I went to Washington once," she said. "The whole high school class went, two years ago. It's a beautiful city and there's so much to do there. Here the only thing you can do is go out on the river. We saw everything in Washington. Arlington National Cemetery and Kennedy's grave. The Smithsonian. The White House. But you know what I remember the most? That big grassy mall by the Lincoln Memorial. There was a man sleeping on one of the grates on the mall, and I said, 'Hey, why doesn't he just go home?' Our teacher said, 'He can't; he doesn't have a home.' Doesn't *have a home*? I couldn't believe it. It was one of the strangest things I've ever seen."

Coming into Harrison, a car passed so closely that it scraped the rearview mirror on the left side of my handlebar. A pedestrian who saw me wobble and finally steady yelled at the driver to slow down. Harrison was built around a central square and had an appearance of permanence. I spent twenty minutes exploring its streets on my bike. Like many small towns, in order to survive, Harrison was trying to remake itself—fixing up the downtown core and, for aesthetic reasons, removing the parking meters—but clearly the transition said a great deal about the troubled state of Main Street, U.S.A. The sixty-five-year-old Spanish-style Hotel Seville at Main and West Ridge Avenue had been turned into a complex of adult apartments. The Lyric Theater, which opened in 1929, two years after talkies debuted, was closed. The Montgomery Ward Building on North Willow now housed little shops and called itself a mall. The two-story Boone County Jail—it provided a residence for the sheriff as well as cells for prisoners until 1976—had become a home for battered and abused women and children.

I pitched up at a Holiday Inn on the far end of town, more extravagant than my usual accommodations but worth the extra dollars, I thought, because the marquee advertised that it had, remarkably enough, a lounge. I walked in about eight o'clock, after doing my laundry, putting some notes in my computer, pumping up my tires and changing into street clothes that were looking increasingly scruffy. The lounge was a dark windowless room, located behind a closed door just off the lobby. "You'll have to sign in if you want a drink," the bartender said. "This is a dry county." That seemed to make no sense whatsoever, but I signed the register and paid a ten-dollar fee that gave me a year's membership, in what, I don't know. The place had none of the congeniality that I find so pleasant in a good tavern. Two men were at the bar, not talking, and four others sat alone at separate tables around the empty dance floor. They drank hard and fast. The place had all the levity of a Saudi Arabian speakeasy. I remarked to the bartender that a dry county must provide a wholesome environment for high school kids to grow up in, without the temptation of beer and liquor.

"They may not do alcohol," he said, "but there's lots of drugs around so it comes out 'bout the same in the end."

9

BETWEEN 1980 AND 1991—WHEN THE DIET BUSINESS WAS IN full bloom—the average adult American put on eight pounds. That, says the National Center for Health Statistics, is the equivalent of an extra one million tons of fat on the waistline of a nation where one in three persons is certifiably over-weight. Ironically, the more we spend trying to get thin— $15 billion a year on diet soft drinks alone, another $4 billion on stuff like Lean Cuisine and pseudo-food appetite suppres-sants—the plumper we become. Something is clearly out of whack. These contradictions were of no concern to me, however, because I had learned the secret of gluttony with-out guilt. Day after day I started the morning with French toast or pancakes, enjoyed apple pie with double scoops of ice cream during pre-noon coffee breaks, drank milk shakes, Hawaiian Punch and chocolate milk by the bucketful, snacked on three or four candy bars in the afternoon and often had room for a hot dog or two before I started think-ing about dinner. Unlike the rest of America, the more I ate, the less I weighed. I could eat two pieces of coconut custard pie at 11 A.M. and within an hour on the road burn off the 450 calories and then some. By the time I reached western

Arkansas, the love handles on my waist had disappeared and I had to tighten my belt an extra notch to keep my pants up.

It occurred to me that the bicycle industry had done a miserable job promoting an image of what biking is all about. Pick up a cycling magazine and what you'll see are pictures of sweat-drenched, overmuscled Zeuses stuffed with carbohydrates, looking as though they were about to die grinding out another mile on their $3,000 bicycles. Experts tell you what to eat, when to go flat-out *up* a hill, how to train. One article I ran across was titled "I Hurt, Therefore I Am," and in another a champion sprinter said of his training regimen: "I push myself to the point where I can barely walk. . . . I push myself to where I throw up." I suppose that's fine if you're prepping for the Olympics, but what about someone like me who doesn't like throwing up and just wants to go out and have some fun biking?

In the early days of the sport in the United States, in the 1880s, there was considerable debate as to whether bicycling was even healthy. Some physicians warned that bicycling could bring on insanity, damage children's nervous systems and create a thirst so great that only beer would quench it, which in turn would lead to kidney stones. They cautioned riders to beware of "bicycle eye"—an alleged strain caused by keeping the eyes constantly raised while the head is in a lowered position—and one skeptic claimed that women who bicycled risked destroying the "feminine organs of matrimonial necessity." Others feared bicycling would affect a woman's pelvic muscles and increase the labor pains of childbirth. Such nonsense passed quickly into folklore and by 1955—the year Schwinn swamped the market with its classic Black Phantom bike and Dwight Eisenhower suffered a serious heart attack—

the President's surgeon, Dr. Paul Dudley White, was touting bicycling as an excellent way for otherwise sedentary people to stay healthy. Soon therapists were recommending it to restore patients' flexibility and physicians were telling people with heart or lung problems, the elderly, diabetics, the overweight and just average Joes who needed some exercise to go out and get a bike.

There were only four staples in our home outside Boston when I grew up in the fifties: pot roast, macaroni and cheese, tuna noodle casserole and chicken à la king. We ate what tasted good and, best as I can remember, didn't worry about what was healthy and what wasn't. Since it is now fashionable not to accept accountability for one's own behavior, I guess I should blame mother and her good home cooking for my continuing pedestrian preferences in food. The fact is, though, that rural America and urban America do not eat the same food and of the two choices, I vastly prefer the menus I found in the small country towns through which I traveled. In nearly fourteen hundred miles I had not seen a piece of romaine lettuce, a leaf of radicchio or any pasta other than spaghetti and meatballs. I was in a land where everyone ate iceberg lettuce with ranch dressing and menus were abundant with great foods that I had thought had vanished from our tables forever: meat loaf, chicken-fried steak, chipped beef, liver and onions, chicken pot pie, mashed potatoes and gravy. Every night was a banquet, and no waitress ever volunteered her name and said she was going to be my server tonight.

I'll admit to being intimidated before leaving home by all the warnings in cycling books about the need for a proper diet. I was told in one that my diet should consist of 65 percent carbohydrates, 20 percent protein and 10 percent fats—

the unaccounted-for 5 percent being a free choice, I guess—
and in another that I had to balance simple, quick-energy carbos (found in raisins, bananas and sugar) with complex carbos
(pasta and legumes). The simple carbos went quickly to the
muscles as body fuel known as glucose. But since the body
can only store a two-hour supply of glucose, I had to "teach"
it to burn fat for energy. It sounded complicated. I tracked
down Mark Jenkins in Montana to seek advice. Jenkins had
climbed on five continents and bicycled across four. He had
just written a book, *Off the Map*, about biking through
Siberia. I asked him if I would really die if I didn't load up on
pasta and fig bars. "No. Listen to your body," he said. "It'll
tell you what you need. You want to eat hamburgers, eat
hamburgers. You get stuck in some town on a rainy day, go
sit at a bar and drink beer and meet the locals. That's half the
fun of what you're going to do." I thought of Jenkins's advice from time to time on the road and I was certain of one
thing: He would have made a great biking companion.

I picked up Route 412 outside Alpena and rode it into
Fayetteville, which was one of only five places in Arkansas I'd
ever heard of before entering the state, the others being Little Rock, Fort Smith, Pine Bluff and Hope. The local paper
carried a story on Thomas Carnes, who had walked out of
Los Angeles twenty-three years ago and was still walking.
Carnes, a Vietnam vet, said he had covered 300,904 miles and
gone coast-to-coast twenty times. The picture accompanying
the article showed him in a camouflage jacket and jeans, carrying small flags for the POWs and MIAs. "I walk in remem-
brance," he said. Remarkably, the reporter neglected to ask
Carnes what he thought of *Forrest Gump*.

Route 412 was being widened and straightened. Bulldozers were punching a new path across vast meadows that would eliminate the loops and meanderings in the old road. Convoys of trailer trucks moved slowly through the construction zones, kicking up clouds of dust that layered my mouth and clung to my nostrils. Ten miles from Siloam Springs on the Oklahoma border, I stopped in a village that soon would be bypassed by the new 412. The village had half a dozen homes scattered back off the road and one commercial enterprise, a defunct gas station and general store that had been turned into a flea market by the elderly owners. A sign outside said, ICE COLD SOFT DRINKS. An old man and his wife were sitting on a sofa, surrounded by shelves and piles and tables of worn farm implements, china, antique lamps, old root-beer bottles, magazines, garden tools, kitchen utensils, tin boxes, used jigsaw puzzles and a large collection of *Reader's Digest* condensed books. I bought two cans of Orange Crush and sat on an empty milk crate next to the sofa. There was no sign they either welcomed or objected to my intrusion. I asked if the village had had more residents when the gas station and general store were last in operation, in the fifties. "Don't suppose there were any more of 'em," he said, "but it'd be hard to know precisely without counting 'em up." He was not pleased with the construction and heavy truck traffic outside. "See, the problem we got in northwest Arkansas is that there're more cars than the roads can handle. We've got no railroad here, so everything moves by truck. Me, I'll be happy when they get that cutoff finished and we're not on the main road anymore. It'll make things a lot quieter here."

"That probably won't help business much, will it?" I said.

"Hell, I don't care about business. I just want it quieter."

I crossed into Oklahoma just before dusk. The sky was orange and appeared to stretch clear to the Pacific. I felt like I owned the world. "California?" the woman in the motel said. "I don't envy you. You've got a long way to go."

"Yeah," I said, "but look how far I've come."

10

THE BICYCLE WAS THE FIRST VEHICLE DESIGNED TO MOVE man without relying on animals or other humans. Though social historians seldom even acknowledge their existence, bicycles a century ago revolutionized travel and recreation in America, affected how we dressed and socialized, and challenged Victorian values: propriety versus pleasure, mature reserve versus youthful exuberance, femininity versus liberation. "These bladder-wheeled bicycles are diabolical devices of the demon of darkness," a Baltimore preacher said from his pulpit one Sunday morning in 1896. "They are contrivances to trap the feet of the unwary and skin the nose of the innocent. They are full of guile and deceit. When you think you have broken one to ride and subdued its wild and Satanic nature, behold, it bucketh you off in the road and teareth a great hole in your pants." Puritan indignation aside, though, most Americans of the 1890s embraced "the wheel" as one of the great inventions of their time, turning the bicycle into a wildly popular fad that transcended age, sex, race and class. *Everyone* was mounting up, and, like the preacher, referring to bicycles in distinctly equine terms. The bicycle was affordable, egalitarian, democratic (unlike trains, in which classes were separated in Pullmans and coaches). When men of all stations in life started pedaling off, shoulder to shoulder, for organized weekend rides, when youngsters and women began heading unescorted into the countryside on their bicycles, a new kind of emancipation that spanned the generations took hold. The bicycle redefined mobility, freedom, proper conduct. Said the Bureau of the Census in Washington: "Few articles ever used by man have created so great a revolution in social conditions as the bicycle."

The roots of America's first national fad went back to the Eastern cities of the late 1870s and the male-only bicycling clubs formed in elegant lodges with reading chambers, attended locker rooms and paneled parlors for sipping brandy and smoking cigars. On weekends the members would gather in brown corduroy uniforms and riding boots, their high-wheel "ordinaries"—or "horseless horses," as they were sometimes called—at their side. Following drill procedures taken from the U.S. Army's cavalry manual, they would count off by twos, mount in unison and pedal off in formation at a bugler's call. Scouts rode ahead to look for dangerous sections of road and for carriages that had to be passed. At the sign of a hazard, the captain would order his bugler to sound "No. 23, Cavalry Tactics" and the club would close ranks and ride in single file, until given the command to "ride at ease." Entire villages turned out to watch the wheelmen sweep by.

By the early 1890s high-wheelers had given way to the

"safety" bicycles we know today and mass production had lowered the cost of a bike to thirty or forty dollars, putting bicycles within reach of the workingman. Annual sales rocketed into the millions; the number of bicycle manufacturers in the United States—some of whom had switched over from producing furniture, carriages and shoes—surpassed four hundred. Newspapers speculated that bicycles would render passenger trains obsolete and become the prime source of transportation. "Walking," commented one journal, "is on its last leg." In one year the American consul in Birmingham, England, reportedly took the entire steel output of Birmingham's mills for bike-frame tubing. *Outing* magazine reported in its February 1896 edition:

> *The cycle trade is now one of the chief industries of the world. Its ramifications are beyond ordinary comprehension. Its prosperity contributes in no small degree to that of the steel, wire, rubber, and leather markets. . . . A decade ago the American steel tube industry was unprofitable. The production of this most essential part of cycle construction has, during the past two years, been unequal to the demand, and even now every high-grade tube mill in this country is working night and day on orders that will keep them busy throughout the year. Nearly every season since 1890 has witnessed a doubling of the number of our factories and a multiplication of the product of a large proportion of the older ones.*

Americans' enthusiasm for the bicycle knew no bounds. Adults serenaded Daisy and her bicycle built for two, packed Madison Square Garden for a six-day continuous bicycle race and made a hit of the Broadway farce *The Bicyclists*. On summer Sundays a hundred thousand New Yorkers poured out of the city on their bicycles, pedaling through Yonkers to the countryside around Tarrytown and White Plains. So great was the exodus that the Ninth Avenue elevated line operated bicycle trains between Rector and 155th Streets on Sunday, with each car having seats on one side of the aisle and bike racks on the other. From Boston to Butte, Montana, bicycle clubs by the hundreds took to the country each weekend on trolleys and trains. Some of the trains attached special dancing cars. In Philadelphia a merchant named Woo Head founded the First Chinese Bicycling Club and Brooklyn saw the formation of a Fat Man's Bicycle Club in which membership was denied to anyone weighing less than 250 pounds. "A few years ago when the 'safety' first made its appearance," said the May 1896 issue of *Munsey* magazine, "the most enthusiastic devotee of the wheel would scarcely have dared to claim for it a place among the great inventions of the age. Today, in reckoning the achievements of the nineteenth century, to such epoch making discoveries as the railroad, the steamship, the telegraph, and the telephone, we can hardly refuse to add, as the latest item on the list, the bicycle."

So great was the bicycle's popularity that noncycling businesses began to suffer. The sale of books and theater tickets plummeted in the cities, tailors and jewelers went out of business, piano sales were cut in half. "What has happened since the bicycle came into popular favor?" said a Chicago piano dealer. "Why, the young people that otherwise would save up for a piano save up for two bicycles instead." The bicycle boom—combined with the introduction of electric trolleys in 1895—also idled 240,000 horses that had pulled trams and passenger wagons in the seven largest Eastern cities. Finding new uses for the bicycle consumed the American imagination. A doctor joined two tandem bikes to a stretcher and used his invention as an ambulance in the streets of Chicago. The Chicago postmaster ran an experiment in which mail was delivered by carriers on horse, bike and foot; the bikers won handily every time. The New York and New Jersey Telephone Company put its inspectors on bikes, and policemen pedaled the streets of Boston, Philadelphia and New York. The Salvation Army mounted a troop of bicyclists to cover Colorado's mining towns. To make riding more comfortable, many cyclists started wearing something American males had always shunned—short pants. *Scientific American* wrote of the bicycle in 1896:

> *As a social revolutionizer it has never had an equal. It has put the human race on wheels, and has thus changed many of the most ordinary processes and methods of social life. It is the great leveler, for not 'til all Americans got on bicycles was the great American principle of every man is just as good as any other man, and generally a little better, fully realized. All are on equal terms, all are happier than ever before, and the sufferers in pocket from this universal fraternity and good will may as well make up their minds to the new order of things for there will be no return to the old.*

The five-mile Coney Island Cycle Path in Brooklyn was so popular with cyclists that six months after its opening, in June 1895, it was widened from fourteen to seventeen feet. Grand plans were laid for a series of bike paths across much of the East and Midwest. Illinois, Wisconsin and Minnesota designed the 530-mile Great Sidepath from Minneapolis to Chicago, and a

Manhattan–Buffalo–Ohio bike path was proposed. Pasadena broke ground in 1898 on an elevated cycleway that would carry bikers, sometimes at heights of fifty feet above street level, along the Arroyo Seco to downtown Los Angeles. The city completed two miles of the structure before the powerful Southern Pacific Railroad, fearing it would lose business on the fifteen-mile Pasadena–Los Angeles run, won an injunction to block continuation of the path. But enthusiasm in cycling had peaked by the turn of the century and the automobile was about to appear in large numbers. Pasadena let the project lapse, then tore down the wooden cycleway. The heyday of the bicycle was over.

Ironically, much of what was in vogue during that halcyon era has returned to fashion in the America of the 1990s. In over six hundred jurisdictions from Boston to Seattle, police departments have mounted up again and are using bicycles for everything from park patrols to drug interdiction. Bike messengers fly through our city streets. Every state has a bicycle coordinator in its highway department and a network of bicycle clubs—twenty-two in California alone—reaches across the country. Los Angeles is putting bike racks on all its twenty-five hundred city buses in an attempt to reduce car traffic. Hundreds of miles of bike paths are under construction in a score of states. Nearly 3 million Americans are commuting to work, at least occasionally, on bicycles. In our search for better, more efficient ways to move, we have, in a manner of speaking, gone full circle and headed ourselves right back toward the 1890s.

11

CROSSING A BORDER IN THE UNITED STATES USUALLY doesn't bring much change. States melt into each other, and for a few miles, anyway, the landscape and the people and the towns look about the same on one side of the line as on the other. But as soon as I slipped into Oklahoma on Route 412, the world appeared distinctly different. The omnipresent Baptist church gave way to discount tobacco shops operated by Native Americans. The land flattened and widened and all about me was an abundance of sky and space and the first vague hints that I was on the doorstep of the West. I saw men wearing Stetsons instead of visored caps and, once again, broken beer bottles on the roadside. Pickups outnumbered cars by a wide margin. In one town, when I couldn't place myself on the map and asked where I was, the woman in the café replied: "Cherokee Nation."

On the maps of the 1870s, this big square chunk of plains was identified as Indian Territory. It marked the easternmost range of America's buffalo herd and was the home of twenty tribes, among them the Southern Cheyennes, who had been driven out of Colorado after clashing with gold miners. Black Kettle, a Cheyenne chief, had shown his loyalty to the United States by flying the American flag over his tepee during a peace council, held near Fort Lyon in 1864 in an attempt to settle the Colorado conflict. The summit ended with a surprise dawn raid on the Cheyenne camp by the Colorado Vol-

unteers. More than a hundred Indians were killed, and Black
Kettle's wife was badly wounded. Eventually Black Kettle led
his remaining followers to a cottonwood forest along the
Washita River in Indian Territory. The Arapahos followed
their Cheyenne friends there and it was against these tribes
that General Philip Sheridan in 1868 turned loose Lieutenant
Colonel George Armstrong Custer with the official order:
"To proceed south in the direction of the Antelope Hills,
thence toward the Washita River, the supposed winter seat of
the hostile tribes; to destroy their villages and ponies, to kill
or hang all warriors, and bring back all women and children."
And it was to Indian Territory that Chief Joseph and his Nez
Percé followers were transported in railroad freight cars in
1878 following a thousand-mile running battle with the U.S.
Army that took them from the Valley of Winding Waters in
Oregon to Montana's Bear Paw Mountains. "Hear me, my
chiefs," Chief Joseph had said when he and his surviving band
of eighty-seven warriors surrendered to the Army. "I am
tired; my heart is sick and sad. From where the sun now
stands, I will fight no more forever." Far from home, in the
hot, arid plains of Indian Territory, Chief Joseph's people
died one by one.

The desolate territory that was part of the Louisiana Pur-
chase in 1803 and became Oklahoma in 1907 has today the
largest Indian population in the United States: more than
250,000 Native Americans representing sixty-seven tribes.
North of Tulsa I turned off the road and into the tribal headquarters of the Pawnees. The reservation has a large hospital
and clusters of tidy small homes and looked not much different than many non-Indian communities I had passed
through. Three young men were hunkered on the steps of

the hospital, smoking, and I stopped to ask about local accommodations. There weren't any, they said. One of the Pawnees, who wore the baggy pants and the backward cap of city kids, offered me a cigarette. He inquired about my journey and seemed confused by my lack of purpose. Why, he asked, would anyone want to bicycle coast-to-coast when he could drive?

I tried to explain the compensation of unexpected encounters along untraveled roads. I mentioned the rush of wind in my face, of being unhurried, of growing stronger, and being close to the land and feeling the rhythm of the road in my bones. "It's just a kick," I said.

"Yeah, but what's the *purpose?*" he asked. "You'd make it faster in a car."

No one else on the entire journey ever asked me why I was soloing a transcontinental route. To me, part of the beauty of the trip was its lack of real purpose. I was merely exercising my right and my need to move and to keep moving. Americans, whether in towns or cities, seemed to understand this as a fundamental expression of the American character: that even if our feet are planted firmly in the soil of home, our dreams are anchored beyond the westward mountains, as were our forefathers'. A garage mechanic back in Tennessee had told me he always wanted to do what I was doing. Then he added, "Course, I'd want to do it on a horse, not a bicycle. I'd go straight across, no roads, no towns, like the settlers did. I don't know what I'd do about all the fences, but I'd figure a way." Maybe it was the romantic in me, but it seemed if anyone should have understood the nature of my journey, it would be a Native American, and I felt saddened that the young Pawnee had proved me wrong.

Route 412 used to be the main east-west route across Oklahoma, but a new toll road—no hitchhikers or bicyclists allowed—now bears that designation and so on the first days of the ride through Oklahoma I was shunted off on what was marked "Scenic 412." The towns along it reminded me of a black-and-white photograph from the forties: Each has a block or so of one-story buildings that includes a bank, café, fraternal lodge and sometimes a shuttered move theater. The highway shoots straight through the town and disappears into the distance where the plains meet the sky. The cafés all bake their own pies and most open at 6 A.M. and close at 2 P.M., on the premise that farmers and ranchers have more important things to do in the afternoon than to talk over coffee. Their rest rooms are identified with labels such as "Hens" and "Roosters" or "Does" and "Bucks." They always caused me a moment's hesitation on entering, and I was never quite sure I had made the right choice until I saw a urinal on the wall.

Conversations came easily in Oklahoma. Again, I was struck by how great the divide between rural and urban American. Our big coastal population centers may set the national agenda, but the quiet voices I heard along forgotten routes carried, I thought, an important message. They were the voices of the other America—an America that is old-fashioned, hardworking, trusting, decent—and if we who live in the cities listened to them more attentively, we would feel better about the country, and ourselves. In Leach most of the town had gathered for a flea market on the soccer field of the elementary school. The students seemed to be running the event and I asked a woman with a strong square face and sky-blue eyes what was going on.

"Oh, the kids are raising money for a class trip to Six

Flags," she said, referring to the Texas theme park. "They've been selling pickles, washing cars, holding bake sales all year. That's my boy over there. We live out by Locust Grove but I've been trucking him here every day since the first grade. The school's got only a hundred twenty children and you seldom get more than twelve or thirteen in a class. My husband and I own the little café down the road. We bought it two years ago. It'd gotten real run-down and they were going to close it up. My husband never let me work before. He'd say, 'Honey, you stay home. Raise the kids. Be a mother. Run the farm. That's your job and it's plenty.' We have a hundred ten acres, with some cattle. Not many. Just about ten. My husband was a trucker, ever since he was seventeen. He's been all over the country. A couple of years ago, he said, 'You know, I think it's time I gave up the road and stayed home a while.' I never thought he'd do it. The road really gets in your blood. But he did quit. Now he's working in the cement factory. Anyway, I always wanted to run a little place, just sandwiches and coffee. The people in Leach didn't want the café to close. So my brother came up from Florida to help out. He bakes the doughnuts. My two girls waitress. I help out. I'm here as much as I can be, with the kids and farm and all. In the mornings we do a real good business. Everyone in town is in the café. We used to be open at night, but it just doesn't pay. The business we got didn't even cover the salary of keeping someone working. Next summer we're going to get an ice cream machine. That may bring people back at night. We used to get people who came off the turnpike for something to eat, but they built a Burger King on the 'pike, so we don't get them anymore. But we're doing all right. It's family. And we do a little side business, delivering doughnuts around. I tell my people, if the road's ever icy, if the snow's too deep, just forget it. Come on home. It's not worth the twenty dollars we get for the doughnuts to end up hurt in a ditch. And I tell them if anyone ever comes in and wants the money from the register, just tell them, 'Take what you want. I won't even remember what you look like.' "

The wind was at my back and I made good time heading out of Leach. It was October now and the first leaves of autumn were falling. The days were crisp but not yet cold. I studied the motion of the tall grass along the roadside to gauge the direction and intensity of the wind. When only the tufted tops wavered, I figured the wind at less than 5 mph, not enough to interfere with my progress; when the stems bent and swayed too, the wind was usually blowing at 10 mph or better and would either speed or slow my journey, depending on its direction. The warmth of the pavement had attracted communities of insects—spiders, ants, caterpillars, worms, crickets and beetles, whose crossing from one shoulder to the other was a perilous one. I had swung off 412 and onto 69, a four-lane highway that carries truckers who want to avoid the interstates from Dallas to Kansas City. I was less timid than I had been at first and held my ground along the far-right white line, figuring the road belonged to me as much as it did to the eighteen-wheelers. I had ridden fifty-nine miles by the time I got to Pryor and it was only 2 P.M. I'd put in an honest day's work and would go no farther. I settled into Pat's Café and Bar, the first twenty-four-hour establishment I'd run into in fourteen hundred miles. On the counter by the cash register was a plastic jug, filled with change and dollar bills. Written in crayon on the jug were the words: DONATIONS FOR THE ALTON O'BAR FAMILY.

I asked the waitress what trouble had struck the O'Bars and she replied, as though no further explanation were necessary, "Vera died. Didn't you hear?"

12

ON THE TWO-LANE ROAD TO CLAREMORE, A COUPLE OF hours' ride from Pryor, my eyes strained to bring into focus a form on the pavement far ahead. It was moving too slowly to be a motorcyclist and too steadily to be a large dog. The form looked shapeless, like a dark blob, and it wasn't until we were within about half a mile of each other that I could make out what was approaching. First I could discern the bulging saddlebags, then the thin frame and wheels, and hunched over the handlebars, a biker, pedaling hard. He drew closer over so gradually and I could tell he was straining. He made for a forlorn sight, a man alone in the roomy, empty landscape, struggling along a deserted road. "Poor bastard," I muttered in sympathy before realizing the irony of my reaction. This is precisely how I must have looked to motorists and I wondered if they whispered similar words as they passed me by.

Except for a few children and an Arkansas farmer with groceries loaded in his wire handlebar basket, I had not seen another biker in more than fourteen hundred miles. I had imagined my first encounter with a fellow tourer would be a joyous one and I pulled to the side of the road to await his arrival. He was a youngish man, probably less than thirty, with an angular, tanned face and bushy eyebrows that made his head appear top-heavy. His rear rack was piled high with a sleeping bag, tent and cooking gear. He rode a mountain bicycle with fat, treaded tires that were more suited for off-road excursions than touring.

"It's good to see another biker," I said. "I thought I was the only one in the world out here doing this. Where are you headed?"

He said he was moving—that's the word he used, *moving,* as in relocating—from Hondo, New Mexico, to Indianapolis. He camped at night in the bushes. We chatted for a few minutes about roads and destinations and logistics, but, it turned out, didn't really have much to say to each other. Maybe we'd both been alone so long we had lost the art of socializing.

"Well, guess I'd better get going," he said. "Good luck."

"You, too."

We mounted up, he heading east, I, west. We met and departed as strangers and it occurred to me that bicycles are great equalizers, capable of concealing all the clues of who we are. A fancy car gives some hint of your financial resources; your seat in an airplane—coach or first—probably says something about your station in life; your choice of clothes reflects whether you're flashy, conservative, sloppy, fastidious. But bicycles give away nothing. They all look about the same regardless of price. Their riders all dress and sweat about the same. They all endure the same hardships on the road. From his appearance and equipment, I could not tell if the man headed for Indiana was rich or poor, a college professor or a high school dropout, an athlete or a duffer. Nor could he have told anything about me; bicycles, like the Greyhound, reduce travel to an egalitarian experience.

In Claremore, where Will Rogers is buried, I crossed for the first time what had been U.S. 66, the Mother Road, as John Steinbeck called it in *The Grapes of Wrath*. Before 66 was replaced by interstates, leaving only scattered, unconnected remnants of the road across the West, the highway skirted the western end of Claremore on its former 2,200-mile journey through three time zones, eight states and fifty-five towns, from the corner of Jackson Boulevard and Michigan Avenue in Chicago to the Santa Monica Pier, where I, too, would end my journey if all went well. The Will Rogers Hotel on 66, once resplendent with radium water baths and a cupola atop the seventh floor that flew the American flag, was boarded up. Two neon signs were still attached to the brick hotel: one said, BATHS, the other, STEAKS, BANQUETS. I got off my bike and peered through the plate-glass windows into the lobby. Most of the furniture had been removed, but the reception desk was intact and I had the sense that the last guest had checked out only yesterday. Around the corner the 11:45 A.M. Greyhound from St. Louis was loading passengers for Tulsa, Oklahoma City, Amarillo, Albuquerque and Los Angeles. I followed the bus out of town but could keep up for only a few blocks.

Ahead, a twenty-seven mile run down Route 20, lay Ski-atook, near the site of an old Cherokee trading post. I had an appointment to keep there with a friend and needed to make the town by sundown. A week earlier I had called the friend, Mark Murphy, at the newspaper where he worked in Fort Worth to inquire about routes through Texas in case snow struck the Rockies. Mark had done some bike touring in the West and beaten cancer and, like myself, had the printer's ink of the newsroom in his veins. He offered to drive the three hundred miles from Fort Worth to bring me supplies and share a few beers if we could figure out a meeting point in Oklahoma. It was an offer that exceeded the bounds of friendship. I told him I'd dearly love company. We agreed I could probably make Skiatook in seven days and we'd meet there.

"How are we going to arrange a place to rendezvous?" I asked, since neither of us knew if Skiatook had a motel or a café or even more than a handful of residents.

"Don't worry. Your job's getting there. Mine's finding you."

Skiatook was bigger than it looked on the map, stretching nearly a mile along Route 20. Lining both sides of the highway when I arrived in midafternoon was an odd sight: a demonstration of five hundred or so people, all white and wholesome-looking and well enough dressed to have just walked out of church. They held small placards that said, ABORTION IS MURDER and JESUS DIED FOR OUR SINS. I rode leisurely through the gauntlet and was surprised to be greeted by silence. "How you doing?" I called out to one fine-looking woman a few feet away. She smiled faintly and did not hold eye contact. The demonstration seemed strangely misplaced in such an out-of-the-way place and as far as I could tell no one in Skiatook was paying it any heed. At the end of town, near a dozen parked buses that had carried the group to Skiatook, I found a $17.95-a-night motel with flush toilets and cable TV. Thirty minutes later Mark knocked on my door. He held a brown grocery bag containing two pints of whiskey, four maps reaching from Texas to California, a sturdy floor pump to inflate my tires, three inner tubes in a Ziploc bag generously sprinkled with talcum powder, a Texas newspaper and a spray can of oil to lubricate my chain. ("A spray can of oil?" Sandy asked when I told her of Mark's gift bag. "Is that a new kind of male bonding?")

Mark had given my route a good deal of thought and he spread the maps out on the bed, suggesting several alternate roads that dropped south and would carry me through flatter, warmer terrain than my planned way along Norty Stewart's orange-marker line. "If you can keep out of the snow," he said, "the only thing you've got to worry about is the Oklahoma Panhandle. It's a couple of hundred miles across and there's nothing there. But I don't see how you're going to avoid it unless you pick up 60 in Seiling and head across Texas." His finger traced the way. There were long, uninhabited stretches along 60, too, and in the end we folded up the maps and decided I should take my chances in the Panhandle and the mountains of northern New Mexico and Arizona. "If you get stuck, you can always hitch a ride," Mark said. I had no qualms about catching a lift if there were a reason to but said I'd have to fess up in anything I wrote.

It was fun being with a friend again and Mark's company made where I had been and where I was going seem a lonely affair. We talked about newspapers and groused that working for them wasn't as much fun as it used to be. ("I guess I sound just like the old-codger editors I heard when I was young," said Mark, who was sixty-one. "They were always saying, 'Papers aren't what they used to be. The heyday is over.' ") We agreed that our passion for major league baseball was ebbing in the wake of a long, dumb strike by millionaire players at odds with billionaire owners. ("Wealthy entertainers on a picket line?" I said. "Come on, why should I care? Baseball used to be a mirror of all that was good in America. Now it's a symbol of the greed.") We drank whiskey from the paper cups in our bathrooms, though neither of us had the drinking capacity we once knew, and after a couple of hours we grew sleepy and I suggested we turn in. It was not quite 10 P.M. The day had been a good one and I was relieved that however self-centered my life had become on the road, I still had more to share with friends than tales of my wandering. Had anyone overheard our conversations, he might have thought we were just a couple of aging guys nostalgic for the days when everything—baseball, newspapers, politics, even the direction of our days—seemed simple and innocent and full of hope. And, of course, he would have been right.

Mark banged on my door at dawn the next morning with a twenty-ounce cup of coffee from the café next door. He pumped up my tires and lubricated my chain with the spray can while I repacked my saddlebags. I was not eager to get rolling. Mark, who biked nearly every day at home, said he had often dreamed of making a transcontinental ride.

"I wish I was going with you," he said.

"So do I."

13

THE KILLING HAD STARTED UP AGAIN IN RWANDA. THE Oklahoma newspapers didn't give it much prominence, other than carrying an occasional wire-service brief, which provided little information except the number of dead. The Rwanda nightmare was so utterly removed from my present life that it was difficult for me to imagine that only four months earlier I had awakened every morning and gone to bed every night with the smell of death all about. It was as though a different me had been in Africa. Here I was, spending my time worrying that triangular little thorns known as goatheads might puncture a tire, and people I had met and liked in Rwanda were spending theirs trying to keep out of range of their neighbors' machetes. I crossed the Arkansas River near the town of Cleveland and memories of another river—the Kagera, which makes its way along the Rwandan border and empties into Uganda's Lake Victoria—returned like an unwelcome visitor. The Kagera was the dumping ground for Rwanda's moment of madness, and when I had last seen it, the river was clogged with bloated, discolored corpses, hundreds upon hundreds of them floating downstream toward Lake Victoria, their appearance as devoid of human character as department store mannequins. One bright, sun-filled morning I had made my way to the Ugandan village of Malembo on the banks of Victoria, twenty miles from any road other than a footpath. The village's fishermen had been detailed by an international relief organization, for six dollars a day each, to pull bodies out of the lake. One after another the power boats returned to shore to unload their ghastly cargo. As bodies were tossed into the trailer of a red tractor for burial in a hand-dug mass grave nearby, John Marembo, the local defense secretary who also served as village record-keeper, dutifully jotted down in his notebook the day's retrieval count: eighteen, nineteen, twenty. . . . Each victim was marked on his pad under a column labeled "Arrivals."

"It is awful enough that Rwanda should have a war like this," Marembo said. "And it is very bad they should give us their litter from the war."

My bike journey, I suppose, would make more dramatic telling had I been in flight from those Rwanda memories. But to suggest there was a relationship between what I did in May and what I was doing in October would not be truthful. I have always managed to maintain emotional distance between myself and what I cover, be it an execution at San Quentin or the murder of Palestinian civilians in Beirut's Sabra and Chatilla refugee camps, and although my job as a professional witness may shape my character and my perceptions of the world, at day's end I can always sleep. So the memories of Rwanda came back not because I was haunted but because the juxtaposition of my two lives reminded me of my good fortune to be, as an accident of birth, an American, free, safe, moving on a whim.

Not much could rattle me. Setbacks were usually no more than minor inconveniences. Every day offered a fresh start. In Pawnee (population 2,197), having ridden fifty-six windy, up-hill miles, I ran out of energy and inquired in the Farmers Insurance office on Main Street about local accommodations. The diminutive office was staffed by a lone woman. "There used to be a motel, but it's closed, I think, maybe for sale," she said. She picked up the phone book, which contained only a couple dozen pages, and I commented how small it was compared to what I used back home. "I know," she said, "and this is for two towns." She started making calls: "Martha, this is Mary Lou. What's the name of that motel? You sure it's closed?" . . . "Jim, I've got a bicyclist here who's tired and needs a place to stay. You suppose the doughnut shop will rent him a room?" . . . "Ed, Mary Lou. Don't we have a bed-and-breakfast in town? It's closed, too?" Finally, after seven or eight calls, she directed me to an abandoned five-unit motel at the edge of town and told me to ask for Teresa. The motel had been transformed into a plant shop, but Unit 5 still had a bed and a black-and-white TV, and Teresa said I could have it for fifteen dollars. Apologizing for the lack of amenities, she found me a plastic glass and filled up a plastic-foam cup with dishwasher soap so I could shower.

By the time I had finished washing my clothes and writing my journal and tending to my bike, it was dark. I detached the headlight from my handlebar to use as a flashlight and headed on foot the half mile to the only place to eat, the Sonic Drive-In. The Sonic had no inside tables and served only at the parking spaces, so I called in my order over a little box and sat on the curb, amid oil drippings, to await my hamburger and fries. When I was a teenager, car-hop restaurants were where you went to pick up girls, but most of the Sonic's customers, who ate their dinners in cars and trucks and chatted with one another through open windows, were families. Several were older women alone. The change said something about the transformation of the American workforce. The number of families with two wage earners soared from 16 million to 30 million between 1960 and 1995. Twenty years ago the average family spent 62 percent of its food bill at the grocery store; now the amount is evenly divided between the grocery store and eating out. At the same time the average workweek is growing longer, having increased between 1983 and 1993 by fifty-six minutes to nearly forty-four hours a week. Clearly big-city Americans have no monopoly on needing to scrap to survive. In the small towns, too, people are rushed for time and struggling to maintain their standard of living. The number of waitresses I met working two jobs and farmers moonlighting in part-time town jobs surprised me, and it surprised me even more that I never heard them whine or complain about what it took to get by.

The day after I "bonked" (as cyclists say when you run out of energy) doing fifty-six miles, I rolled off eighty-four and felt fit enough to do another hundred. As far as I could tell, there hadn't been any difference in my diet, the amount of sleep I'd had, the terrain or the weather. I couldn't explain it any more than I could explain why some days I was productive at work and others I wasn't. My route through Oklahoma moved along a high, flat plateau. In the adjacent fields oil derricks stood like prehistoric birds. Sometimes their long steel necks bobbed slowly up and down, joints squeaking and rumbling, but most were motionless, a reminder that the oil boom was no more. The grain silos of Enid (population 50,000, the largest town between Memphis and Albuquerque on my route) appeared on the horizon from a distance of ten miles. Local legend has it that Enid—dine spelled backward—got its name from an illiterate café owner, but I was told that is not true; the Enids were an early settler family. Scores of towns I passed through in the Sooner State were, like Enid, founded on the same date, September 16, 1893, the day thousands upon thousands of settlers lined up, twenty miles away, on horseback and on foot, in buck wagons and carriages, awaiting the pistol shot at noon that would set off their mad dash for free land. A man who jumped the starting gun and staked his claim to a 160-acre plot ahead of more orderly settlers was known as a "sooner." In Enid I found a bar where the TV was broadcasting the weekly city commission meeting. I ordered an extra-day martini, straight up. The bartender served it in a gin-and-tonic glass, awash in vermouth, with a large slice of lime. I did not try another martini in Oklahoma.

The sky was full of lightning and thunder that night and sheets of rain pounded against the windows of my motel room. I fell asleep watching the national weather channel and although it reported the pollen count in Georgia, interstate road conditions in California and the movement of a low-pressure area over the Rockies, I never did get a forecast for Oklahoma. At home weather was of little interest to me, because it didn't affect my routine at all. But on a bicycle, miles from anywhere, weather alone often determined whether my day would be miserable or delightful. It affected my speed and how much water I should carry. It controlled me as it never had in the city, and rather than opening my morning newspaper to the sports page as I used to do, the first thing I read on the road was the weather report. The *Enid Daily Eagle* predicted clearing skies, and, despite a covering of dark, billowing clouds that looked low enough to touch, I set off the next morning with my record intact—not a drop of rain had fallen on me in sixteen hundred miles. Route 412 widened into four lanes through Enid and just out of town, on the other side of the divider, I spotted an Oklahoma Highway Patrol substation. I made a U-turn. During the past month I had phoned various highway patrol offices half a dozen times to check on road conditions and what towns had motels and where I could find a meal. The dispatchers were full of information, and when I said I was on a bicycle, the businesslike edge in their voices disappeared and they'd be so helpful I almost felt as though I'd done them a favor by calling.

"A bicycle?" the dispatcher in the Enid substation said. "Goodness, that must be some way to get around. You're not going to pass much where you're going. Twenty-five miles from here, you'll come to Orienta, where the road forks. There's a grain silo and Qwik gas station just beyond the fork. That's about it. You better get a sandwich at the station, because there's nothing for the next forty-two miles, till Mooreland. Mooreland has an old motel but you're better off getting to Woodward. A bigger town, more motels. And keep an eye on the weather. Storms have a way of coming up out of nowhere this time of year in Oklahoma."

Fighting headwinds all the way and averaging little better than eight miles an hour over the course of eighty-seven miles, I limped into Woodward, on the doorstep of the Panhandle, at 7:30 P.M., lights on, my three water bottles empty. The skies had cleared and the stars were bright as candles. It was a good portent for the morrow.

14

HEADING WEST OUT OF WOODWARD, THE LAST TOWN YOU reach before the Oklahoma Panhandle is Fort Supply on the northern branch of the Canadian River. I stopped to put ice in my water bottles and buy some bananas and candy bars.

The fort was once the frontier outpost for General Philip Sheridan's campaign against the Plains Indians, its supplies and ammunition hauled in from Dodge City, Kansas, in wagon trains that stretched for two miles. In 1908, the Indians conquered, the fort was rebuilt and expanded into a mental hospital and, more recently, was enlarged to include a detention center. A sign on the road by Sheridan's old headquarters advises: HITCHHIKERS MAY BE ESCAPING INMATES.

Twenty miles from Fort Supply, another sign welcomes you to the Panhandle as though you have crossed a state border. The Panhandle is a perfectly shaped rectangle, 34 miles wide, 167 miles long, that on the Indian Territory maps, from 1866 to 1889, was identified as No Man's Land. The desolate strip fell outside all governmental jurisdiction. Unwanted by anyone but its outlaw and cowboy settlers, the Panhandle eventually was patched onto Oklahoma when none of the other adjoining states—Kansas, Colorado, New Mexico, Texas—showed interest in claiming it. I figured it would take me three days to cross, and I was not surprised to learn that the country's rodeo bronc-rider champs in 1991, 1992 and 1993 were from the Panhandle's Texas County. With arctic winters, winds that are never still, and forty or fifty miles between cafés, much less towns, this is not a place that caters to the meek.

The road was empty, save for an occasional cattle truck moving at breakneck speed, and I rode the yellow line down the center of Route 3. Maybe, I thought, this is what Siberia looks like. No trees stood on the depopulated plain and in the fields, amid browning stalks of harvested wheat, idle tractors seemed to have been abandoned at a moment's notice. Every mile or so, I could make out, well back from the road, a home, surrounded by a windbreak cluster of cottonwoods. Pickups were parked outside the houses, but I saw no people, no dogs, no smoke curling from chimneys. I wondered where the kids went to school and how the women did their shopping and what Christmas Day is like when your property reaches as far as the eye can see and there's not another human being in sight. The wind was cold and steady and I pulled off the road and put on my long-sleeved nylon jacket and leggings for the first time since leaving Virginia. On my left, several wooden signs attached to a fence post pointed down a narrow road that ran to the horizon. They said: CEMETERY 1/2 MI S and ROGERS RANCH 2 MI S 1 MI E and BAPTIST CHURCH 1 MI W 1 MI N.

Wind gusts twice blew me off the road. They came with a dull whistle off the plain and bent the grass to the ground. Sometimes the wind paused, as though to catch its breath, but it never really stopped. Biking into it was like trying to advance on an exercise bicycle. I stopped along the road for lunch—water, two bananas and a cigarette—and a sudden blast toppled my bike from its kickstand and sent it crashing to the ground. "What if I break down out here?" I said aloud. "There's not a bike shop for three hundred miles in any direction." But the only damage was to the mirror on my handlebar. Dark clouds swirled overhead. Did it snow in October in the Panhandle? I wasted no time on lunch and moved out, keeping low as possible over the bike. According to a study I had read in *Bicycling* magazine, a cyclist's body accounts for 70 percent of wind resistance; the more aerodynamic I could make myself, the easier the going would be. To maintain a pace of 18 miles an hour in the face of a 10-mph headwind, I needed to exert twice the energy demanded to bike at the same speed through calm air. If someone had drawn an imaginary circle around me, any wind blowing through the forward 200-degree arc would work to slow my progress; only wind from the trailing 160 degrees offered assistance. So my goose was cooked. The prevailing winds would prevail. If only I had been moving with them, west to east, but I had known the risks when I set off: I was leaving home dangerously late in the season and I was heading the wrong direction to take advantage of the winds. A hand-lettered poster tacked to a fence said, GOD IS ONLY A PRAYER AWAY. It seemed worth a try. "Lord," I said, "I'd sure appreciate You turning this wind around and putting it at my back." The wind fell quiet for but a second, then picked up again, as persistent and annoying as a swarm of mosquitoes that follows your every step. I hobbled into the town of Slapout thinking some smart promoter could make a go of a Tour de Panhandle.

Except for a combination gas station/convenience store, Slapout (population six) is a ghost town. The grocery store is boarded up and Fred's Café has been abandoned since Fred's health failed and his relatives moved up from the city to save the place but couldn't manage to scratch out a living. Slapout has only one claim to notoriety: It is the halfway point each summer in the world's longest and most grueling bicycle race, a 2,910-mile heart-stopper from Irvine, California, to Savannah, Georgia, that the winner grinds out in just over eight days. "Some of the cyclists that come through don't even speak English, and to hear a foreign language in Slapout, that's really something," said the woman who runs the gas station. But *eight* days? For four thousand years the speed of traffic on roads changed hardly at all. Abraham of the Old

Testament could get where he was going just about as fast as could George Washington. Conestoga wagon trains covered only two or three miles an hour on their westward journeys and even stagecoaches in the 1830s were hard-pressed to average eight miles an hour. Now we're going coast-to-coast on a bicycle in eight days? That took some pondering: From the East Coast to Slapout had taken me thirty-six days, maintaining what I thought was a steady, workmanlike pace. And the Race Across America cyclists—take note: These people, including a sixty-one-year-old retired CEO and a Vietnam vet amputee with artificial legs who said, "Life goes on. Go out and enjoy it," are *cyclists,* not mere *bikers*—would make it from Slapout to the East Coast in four days. Either I was a wimp or they were insane. I preferred to believe the latter.

Traveling with pace cars and support vans and riding eighteen to twenty hours a day, the cyclists had rolled through Slapout two months before I did. One pace car was emblazoned with the words DEATH BEFORE DNF (Did Not Finish). Some riders wore battery-powered electrical stimulators to ease back pain, others, harnesses to reduce neck spasms. One man's neck was supported by a full body brace. The winner rode the final 375 miles into Savannah nonstop, having been tricked by his crew: He was awakened in his support van for the last leg and told he had had his allotted two hours' sleep. Actually he'd been sleeping for only twenty minutes, but his mind took the bait and his restored body pushed on, even though at the end he said he had no recollection at all of having cycled the final miles.

I felt less overwhelmed by the Panhandle after seeing the photos and clippings of the race the woman in the gas station had given me. I put them back in the manila envelope and asked if the wind was apt to die down in the afternoon. "Sometimes it does, sometimes it doesn't," she said. "Likely as not, it'll blow all day and right through the night." The miles blurred. It was like crossing Australia's Nullarbor Plain, which I had done years earlier in the engine of a train. For 750 miles the track ran straight as an arrow and, lest he get lulled into slumber, the engineer had to push a red button on his control board every forty-five seconds; if he didn't, the train's emergency brakes would engage automatically. Route 3 has no more bends than the Nullarbor tracks and from any given point I could follow the ribbon of pavement for four or five miles with my eye. The road's emptiness and the hum of my tires upon it were hypnotic, causing me to weave and lose concentration. An eighteen-wheeler rumbled up from behind and I wasn't even aware of its presence until the driver rattled me with a blast of his air horn. I veered back onto my edge of the right-hand lane, feeling incompetent, and could not make out what the driver yelled as he sped by and finally, a long way off, disappeared from sight. *Life* magazine in the fifties called Route 50 across Nevada "the loneliest road in America," but by the time I'd spent a night in Elmwood, and another in Guymon, I decided *Life*'s editors had gotten it wrong: The label belonged to Oklahoma's Route 3.

Everywhere I stopped pictures of John Wayne stared at me, just as those of Robert E. Lee had in Virginia. They were on the walls of cafés, in motel lobbies, pasted to gas station cash registers. Teddy Roosevelt was much in evidence, too, and one four-by-six-foot, unsigned painting of him seemed to fill up an entire restaurant in Guymon. Next to it a plaque quoted his 1899 comment: "Far better to dare mighty things, to win glorious victories, though checkered with defeat, than to take rank with those poor souls who neither enjoy much nor suffer much, for theirs is a twilight existence that knows neither victory nor defeat."

On the sixty-one-mile stretch from Guymon to Boise City there is only one community, Four Corners, and in Four Corners there is only one occupied house and one commercial enterprise, a café with sporting goods and hardware supplies in front and tables in back. It's a family-run place whose hearty Sunday buffet is known for miles around (all you can eat, $5.25, or $3.65 if you're over sixty-two). I left my bike unlocked outside and walked in, right on time for the buffet. A dozen elderly ranchers and farmers were at the tables with their wives, dressed as if for church, the men in jackets and string ties, the women in dresses. Two wore high heels. Everyone knew everyone and conversation was animated. Only the man who owned the café with his wife wore overalls. He held a flyswatter in his one hand—he had lost his left arm in a farming accident when he was eight—and was stalking the room in search of flies. Thwack! The swatter came down on the edge of one table. "Got two that time," he announced, and the couple at the table nodded appreciatively. My chicken-fried steak, mashed potatoes, sausage, homemade rolls and chocolate cake had enough calories to last me to California and when I walked outside to keep from dozing off at the table, the owner followed me to my bike and we started talking. He and his sons farmed four thousand acres in addition to running the café, he said, but he doubted that towns like Four Corners would ever prosper again.

"I guess you'd be right calling us a ghost town," he said. "There used to be another café there, across the road, but it burned down, and that structure over there was a gas station.

The fella that ran it died 'bout ten years ago. The fella that built the brick house couldn't make a go of things and he moved on. He's bartending somewhere or other, last I heard. Our place was empty too until my wife and I bought it and fixed it back up as a café. The empty homes you see around, they were the farmers that moved to town—Boise City, Guymon, wherever—for steady jobs. They farmed all they could and when their kids left there was more work than they could handle. I don't suppose the town'll ever come back the way it was, but you don't really know. There's talk of widening the road into four lanes and if they get that hog-processing plant in Guymon going good, we could get trucks rolling through here again. Course, you don't know if you'll get any more traffic on four lanes'n you do on two."

Because the wind didn't become truly unruly until about 10 A.M., I had been getting an early start each morning, and I left Four Corners for Boise City, the westernmost Panhandle town, with five hours of daylight to spare. With Oklahoma's western border within reach, my spirits reached eight on a scale of one to ten. Yesterday they rated a two. Though normally even-tempered to a fault, I found my mood swinging wildly on the road and experienced an elation at day's end that was quite unlike anything I knew at home. Workdays there usually drew to a quiet, unemotional close, marked by the clock. Now, when the last pedal stroke had been taken at an undetermined hour, I was filled with a sense of accomplishment that made me almost giddy. What I had achieved each day was unmistakably defined on the map and odometer. There was no question of how others would judge my work or whether what I had done had merit. I had only myself to please. As if I were a salesman or a road builder, there was a balance sheet at the end of every day, and mine was always in the plus column because each mile brought me closer to my destination.

Since crossing into Oklahoma I had climbed from an elevation of 600 feet to 4,165 feet at Boise City. The wind still blew and the land stayed empty, but now that it was nearly behind me, the Panhandle no longer seemed a hostile place. There is a beauty in its austerity and loneliness that sticks in your mind like a scrapbook photograph. Boise City (population 1,700) seemed to have been plopped down on Route 3 for no particular reason and I biked the length of the town, then turned back to a motel that was within walking distance of a café and convenience store. I napped, spread my Oklahoma and New Mexico maps end to end on the bed and watched The Weather Channel. An early winter storm was threatening the Rockies. I stepped outside. Route 3 was deserted, except for three cattle trucks parked on the wide shoulder. It was sunset. The sky was everywhere and seemed to rise right out of the ground where I stood. Neon lights down the way summoned travelers with flickering promises of EAT and STAY WITH US. A dog barked. Four teenagers cruised by in an old Chevy. Clumps of tumbleweed bounced helter-skelter across a vacant lot. It grew darker. I felt as though I had stumbled onto a movie set for *The Last Picture Show*.

THREE

Into Texas
and on to California

Every time I see
an adult on a bicycle,
I no longer despair
for the human race.
—H. G. Wells

1

THE TOWNSMAN CAFÉ IN BOISE CITY WAS ACROSS THE parking lot from my motel. I walked in holding a plastic bathroom cup full of whiskey and ice. The only other customer was a trucker at the counter, who wore cowboy boots and a T-shirt that said LIFE IS LIKE DEATH IN SLOW MOTION. I took a booth and spread out my maps, still looking for a route that would steer me away from the barren, mountainous expanses of northern New Mexico and the emptiness of Arizona's "Indian Country." There was a way through a corner of Texas and into Albuquerque that looked workable, but that would mean riding the New Mexico interstates, which is illegal for bicyclists. "Chicken-fried steak's on special tonight, and meat loaf," the waitress said. She looked at my cup on the table. "That isn't a cocktail, is it?" she asked. I allowed that it was. "You'd do me a favor taking it back outside," she said. "The thing is, I'm an alcoholic. A recovering alcoholic. It's two years this week I've been sober. I'd feel a lot better if it wasn't around."

"Fair enough," I said, and set the cup outside, under a vending machine for the weekly *Boise City/Cimarron County News*. The waitress shuffled over a while later with my dinner. "Thanks," she said. "The extra potatoes, they're on me."

Darkness fell quickly over the Panhandle and as I was getting ready to pay my bill, two beaten-looking women walked in from the ice-black night, in leggings and yellow rain slickers. "We're frozen. Do you have any soup?" one of them asked. "We just came seventy-five miles. On bicycles." The waitress said: "You oughta talk to that fella in the booth. He's on a bicycle, too." They looked at me. I looked at them. We shared a common thought: Come on, no one else is biking through the Panhandle this time of year. I brought my coffee to the counter to join them. Norma Witherbee and Evie Weber were sisters and real estate agents, about my age, maybe a little older. They were on vacation, biking from their home in Chicago to Anaheim, near Los Angeles, and a better pair of troopers I have seldom met. Their bicycles were seven or eight years old and their gear wasn't high-tech or as spiffy as mine, but when they talked about visiting Vancouver and New Orleans and a lot of places in between, they had gotten there by bicycle. Flats, breakdowns, rain, wind, dogs, getting stranded on country roads and having to pedal until midnight—nothing seemed to faze them. On this trip, they were raising money for the Special Olympics and they passed out donation cards as they went. Norma's nonbiking husband didn't like her being gone two or three weeks at a stretch, and worried about the two of them alone on the road, but on several occasions she had overheard him telling friends about her latest expedition, so she assumed that, though he never said as much, he was rather proud of what his dauntless wife accomplished.

We talked, mostly about routes west and how long it would take to get to this town or that, until the café closed at 9 P.M. Another truck driver had settled in at the counter. He hauled out a thick book of maps and volunteered: "It's getting cold in the Rockies. Eagle Nest was 29 degrees this morning, I heard. Hell, I wouldn't take my rig up there this time of year, much less a bicycle. Let me get the right page. Now look. You take 385 into Dalhart, pick up 54 and head west right here . . ." That was the same route, through Texas, that had caught my eye earlier, and as far as I was concerned, the matter was settled. I penciled in a new, more southerly line to California on my map, roughly following what had been the old U.S. 66. Norma, Evie and I agreed we'd meet after breakfast and bike together to Dalhart. We got up to leave and the truck driver said, "Can I ask you people something? . . . Is what you're doing any *fun?*"

I overslept the next morning and never did link up with the sisters, and, in a way, I was relieved. The thought of biking with strangers made me uneasy. What if they wanted to go faster than I did? What if I ran out of conversation by the first coffee break? What if they broke down? Was I obligated to stick around at the cost of my own pace? And there was one other minor consideration: Bicycle saddles can do embarrassing things to a man. I had, for instance, read letters in cycling magazines from readers seeking advice on how to avoid penile numbness and involuntary ejaculations. Neither was a problem for me, but sitting on a bicycle seat six or seven hours a day did make me need to urinate more often than usual, and I liked the freedom of being able to take a leak along an empty road without having to search out a bush in the name of propriety. So I set off for Texas alone, not unhappily, my Oklahoma map retired to the bottom of my saddlebag. I expected to see Norma and Evie on the road ahead or catch their reflection in my rearview mirror, but they were nowhere in sight.

There are no towns, no gas stations, no restaurants and damn few houses on the daylong ride from Boise City to Dalhart. I wondered how people could live by choice in such woebegone places and the voice of a woman I had met in the Panhandle came floating back to answer my question: "My husband and I went down to Tyler, Texas, the other weekend for a holiday. They had twenty-seven thousand people there. Twenty-seven *thousand*! I couldn't believe it." (Actually Tyler has seventy-five thousand residents.) I asked her if she didn't sometimes yearn for a little more activity than a town with a score of residents offered, and she said, "No way at all. The way it is here, I know everybody. You need a hand, anyone will extend it. You get into a big place like Tyler, and that's just not going to happen."

Seventeen miles from Boise City, Highway 385 makes a bend to the right and at the curve stands a large wooden sign on which is chiseled a single word in foot-high letters: TEXAS. Other states mark their borders with greetings from the governor or state mottoes. Texas needed just a word to deliver its message. I liked the brashness of the premise; anything else on the sign would have been overkill. I probably imagined it but almost instantly the land seemed to become bigger, the cattle herds greater, the wind stronger. The two-lane road was mine alone and I chose the yellow line down the middle.

I made it into Dalhart by two-thirty and welcomed the

thought of going no farther. With a population of seven thousand, Dalhart felt, in comparison to where I'd been, big enough to be the home of a major league baseball team. Four highways converged on the town and trucks and trains rumbled through like convoys, going to Cheyenne on 87, and from El Paso to Chicago on 54, and Odessa to Rapid City on 385 and back toward Oklahoma on 297. I found a sandwich shop near the train tracks. I leaned my bike against the plate-glass window. A group of cowboys in Stetsons, blue jeans and boots eyed me from their table by the kitchen as I walked in, feeling quite out of place in my shorts, helmet and sweaty jersey. I ordered coffee and a grilled cheese sandwich and, leaving my wallet and reading glasses on the table, went back outside to buy a newspaper.

"That's a pretty good way to get your money stole, wouldn't you say?" one of them drawled when I returned.

"Back in Washington, D.C, it is," I said, trying my best diplomacy, "but I figured in West Texas it's safe." They beamed and I knew I had won them over.

"Glad to hear you Easterners know Texas is different," he said. "You'll find pretty decent, honest people out here. . . . What do you think of Texas so far?"

"Well, I've only seen about thirty miles of it, but it's, ah, impressive." They nodded in unison.

Later, after the cowboys had left, I went to pay my bill and the woman at the cash register said, "The gentlemen that was at the corner table already took care of it."

I spent the afternoon walking around Dalhart, looking at photographs of the Dust Bowl that hung in store windows and on café walls. They showed thick black clouds towering over the town like tidal waves and merchants with shovels standing knee-deep in powder-fine dust and ranches as stark and lifeless as a tundra. It's amazing anyone stayed on to farm and raise a family. That night, in a deserted restaurant, I felt a rush of wind when the door opened. I looked up. It was the sisters from Chicago. They had just made it to Dalhart, six hours after I'd arrived. They'd had a couple of flats, blown a tire off the rim using a gas station air pump in Boise City, tried without success to repair Norma's wobbly saddle, stopped to photograph tarantulas along the highway, biked through two hours of darkness—and were in the most cheerful of spirits. "We got to talking," one of them said. "You were in street clothes last night and we didn't see your bike anywhere, and when you didn't show up this morning, we thought maybe you'd just made it up. That you weren't on a bicycle at all." Norma and Evie were good company and we agreed, again, to meet at breakfast and bike together into New Mexico.

2

THE BICYCLE SEEMS AN UNLIKELY SYMBOL OF WOMEN'S LIBeration, but a century ago, in 1886, when a young American named Margaret Valentine Le Long bicycled alone from Chicago to San Francisco in two months, carrying only an extra skirt and underwear, toilet articles and a pistol, it was precisely that—as bold a statement of feminist independence as burning the bra would be in the 1960s. Riding a bicycle, many nineteenth-century Americans believed, was a manly pastime, an activity that no woman of refinement would even consider. The reasons were many: Some argued that bicycling would destroy "feminine symmetry and poise" and affect pelvic muscles, thus increasing the labor pains of childbirth. Others said women would by sexually stimulated by the saddle. Beyond that, there was the simple question of morality. A senior Chicago police official warned of "contamination" when "women of refinement and exquisite moral training addicted to the use of the bicycle are not infrequently thrown among the uncultivated and degenerate elements of both sexes." On proper dress, the League of American Wheelmen advised women to abandon skirts in favor of trousers. "It is not enough to wear trousers under a short skirt," the league said. "The skirt is lifting with every wind more or less, and attracting curious eyes."

Women had tried tricycles when the big-wheeled penny-farthing bikes captivated the fancy of American men in the 1870s, but the three-wheelers never really caught on and the few women who tricycled alone were often verbally abused by pedestrians and horsemen. The solution, *The Wheelman* magazine advised, was for women to find a male companion: "In this way the lady learns with ease; she is provided with a suitable escort; and if anything goes wrong, she has assistance at hand." The 1880s turned bicycling into a sport more popular than baseball, boxing or horse racing, and turned the attention of manufacturers to how to exploit the untapped market of millions of women. In 1888 the first bicycle with a dropped top-tube to accommodate riders with skirts hit the market. In 1889, Starley Brothers began mass-producing the first women's "safety" bike, a model called the Psycho Ladies' Bicycle. In 1894, Albert Pope, the bicycle manufacturer from Hartford, started featuring bloomer-clad female riders in his advertisements. A West Virginia man sold Cherry's Screens—a shield resembling large bat wings attached to the front of bikes to block the view of women's legs and ankles—and another company offered all-black "mourning bicycles" to attract widows. *Outing* magazine suggested women sew weights into their hems and wear leather-lined skirts lest anyone catch a glimpse of their legs and undergarments in a stiff wind. If ever so slowly, bicycling was losing its gender affiliation.

Speaking of the increasing number of women "awheel," the popular *Munsey* magazine reported in 1896:

> *It is as though a new language had been given to her, and the books of its literature opened before her. Hitherto a weak, helpless creature, she can at her own sweet will cover great stretches of country without appreciable fatigue, and all the delights of motion, sun, and air come without any more effort than has been given to dawdling about the streets. . . . The wheel means too much to woman, when it is fully appreciated and enjoyed, to be considered lightly, or trifled with. It is the best gift that the nineteenth century has brought her.*

The feminist movement was taking root in the United States about that time, and Susan B. Anthony, the seventy-six-year-old activist for women's suffrage, said of the bicycle in an interview with the *New York World:* "I think it has done more to emancipate women than anything in the world." The boldest reformers of the day dared play billiards or order a beer at the bar. Others referred to God as "She." Many argued "rational dress" should replace corsets that gripped the waist with wire fingers and turned figures into hourglasses. And indeed, because of the cycling craze, skirts did become shorter and bloomers—short, full pants fastened at the knee with drawstrings, similar to the knickerbockers men wore—became popular. The corset was fading into history. But women still had to battle for their independence on the bicycle, and the propriety of bloomers was hotly argued.

In Chicago, the police department closed down a "bloomer dance" and threatened to treat women in bloomers as prostitutes. A group of males in Norwich, New York, formed an Anti-Bloomer Brigade and vowed not to associate with women in bloomers. Some small communities forbade bloomer-clad women from bicycling in their streets, and the mayor of Chattanooga proposed an ordinance to keep bloomers off the streets because they were a menace "to the peace and good morals of the male residents of this city." In Flushing, Long Island, three female teachers were ordered by the school board not to ride their bikes to school. When the board met to consider the women's objections, board member A. W. Reimer revealed the real reason for the prohibition:

It is not the proper thing for ladies to ride the bicycle. They wear skirts, of course, but if we don't stop them now they will want to be in style with New York women and wear bloomers. Then how would our schoolrooms look with the lady teachers parading about among the girls and boys wearing bloomers. They might as well wear men's trousers. I suppose it will come to that, but we are determined to stop our teachers in time, before they go that far.

Women bicyclists, however, persevered, and in finally winning acceptance to venture off into the countryside unescorted, in bloomers instead of billowing skirts, they struck a blow for the rights of women everywhere. Many of the nation's leading women of the day became bicycle advocates, including Frances E. Willard, a reformist and president of the Woman's Christian Temperance Union. She took up biking at the age of fifty-three, while suffering from bad health and exhaustion following years of traveling, lecturing and organizing. In her later writings the mastery of the bike became a metaphor for life itself, and the qualities needed to master it, she contended, were the same ones required to advance reforms: steadiness, confidence, determination, discipline. She wrote a book about bicycling and her bicycle, nicknamed Gladys, published in 1895 under the title, *A Wheel Within a Wheel:*

> *I began to feel that myself plus the bicycle equaled myself plus the world, upon whose spinning wheel we must all learn to ride, or fall into the sluiceways of oblivion and despair. That which made me succeed with the bicycle was precisely what had gained me the measure of success in life—it was the Spirit that led me to begin, the persistence of will that held me to my task, and the patience that was willing to begin again when the last stroke had failed. And so I found high moral uses in the bicycle and can commend it as a teacher without pulpit or creed. He who succeeds, or, to be more exact in handing over my experience, she who succeeds in gaining the mastery of such an animal as Gladys, will gain the mastery of life, and by exactly the same methods and characteristics. . . . One of the first things I*

learned was that unless a forward impetus were given within well-defined intervals, away we went into the gutter, rider and steed. And I said to myself: "It is the same with all reforms: sometimes they seem to lag, then they barely balance, then they begin to oscillate as if they would lose the track and tumble to one side; but all they need is a new impetus at the right moment on the right angle, and away they go again as merrily as if they had never threatened to stop at all."

Bicycles helped bring to an end the era of the Victorian woman, and without its trailblazers willing to endure taunts and ridicule, perhaps I never would have met Norma Witherbee and Evie Weber on the road to Texas. Bloomers lost their popularity by the turn of the century, and so did bicycling in general, but the social impact of the "wheel" had been profound. As the English novelist and playwright John Galsworthy wrote:

The bicycle . . . has been responsible for more movement in manners and morals than anything since Charles the Second Under its influence, wholly or in part, have wilted chaperons, long and narrow skirts, tight corsets, hair that would come down, black stockings, thick ankles, large hats, prudery and fear of the dark; under its influence, wholly or in part, have bloomed weekends, strong nerves, strong legs, strong language, knickers, knowledge of make and shape, knowledge of woods and pastures, equality of sex, good digestion and professional occupation—in four words, the emancipation of women.

3

THE TWO SISTERS FROM CHICAGO AND I LEFT DALHART early to take advantage of a lull in the morning winds. Evie asked what my wife thought of me heading off across Texas with two strange women and I said, "I talked to Sandy last night. She thinks it's great I have company." That was true, but it was also true that Sandy was starting to feel abandoned. From mile one, my caper had been a flight that involved no one but me, stood to enrich no one but me. It was easy to forget that the routine of life went on at home and that there was more to the world than the narrow ribbon of pavement I followed. It was Sandy's birthday and I was two thousand miles away. The cat was sick. The downstairs toilet was broken. The weekly paychecks had stopped. And while I had little to concern myself with other than what route I took and where I spent the night, Sandy was knocking heads with deadlines on a film project that had her working weekends and into the nights. "You never ask what's going on in *my* life," Sandy said one evening after I had babbled on about headwinds and my relief at escaping the Panhandle. She was right. I was becoming like a professional baseball player, so self-absorbed and enamored with his accomplishments that he doesn't comprehend the insignificance of his work. I promised Sandy I'd broaden my horizons but wasn't sure I was capable of keeping my word.

"Why don't we draft. It'll cut down on the headwinds,"

Evie said. I didn't know what she was talking about. She pulled ahead and positioned herself so that I was just behind her right shoulder, her rear wheel no more than two inches from my front wheel. "What you have to do is concentrate and stay just off my rear wheel," she said. "If I'm going to turn, to avoid something in the road or whatever, I'll signal by dropping my left or right hand." On an imaginary clock the wind was blowing from the 11 o'clock position and I was at Evie's 5 o'clock. Trying to match her pace while focusing on her wheel rather than the road was distracting but wonderfully effective: She had become a windshield and I was biking effortlessly through calm air. We took turns drafting for each other for ten or twelve miles. Each time I looked into my rearview mirror Norma had fallen behind, her wobbly seat having turned the day into a painful ordeal. We'd wait for her to catch up and, never having learned the art of complaining, she'd say, "Okay, I'm fine. Let's go." We went on, with me drafting in the lead position, the three of us trying to stay close, then the tire Norma had fixed that morning in Dalhart started losing air.

"Drafting isn't going to work," Evie said. "Norma can't keep up with a broken seat. Why don't you go on?"

I did. We said we'd look for each other in Logan or Tucumcari or wherever that day's road ended. I did not feel I was deserting them because, though unspoken, the three of us knew that they were a team and I was on my own. We rode together only by chance. At any fork, each of us was free to say, "I think I'll go this way." In my mirror, farther down Route 54, I caught a last view of them, their yellow slickers vivid against the brown plain, Evie in the lead, Norma close behind, each in perfect pace with the other.

Just before Nara Visa, I crossed into New Mexico and entered the Mountain Time Zone. The days were getting shorter and by six-thirty each evening the sun had dipped below the horizon and it was time to get off the road. Nara Visa had a truckers' café, a run-down motel and half a dozen boarded-up homes and shops. An aging waitress sat at the counter of the café, chain-smoking. I asked her why the town had been mostly abandoned and she said, "I wouldn't know. It's looked like this the three years I been here." According to my rating system, borrowed from baseball's minor leagues, Nara Visa was a Rookie League town. Triple-A towns had a Wal-Mart, a Radio Shack and a choice of fast-food franchises; Double-A, a Radio Shack and at least one franchised restaurant but no Wal-Mart; Single-A, only a Hardee's or a McDonald's. Rookie League towns were at the bottom and weren't much more than outposts. I found a patch of grass outside the café and, although it was tarantula season, stretched out and took a nap, using my helmet for a pillow.

Route 54 cuts 121 miles off the interstate trip from the Mexican border at El Paso to Chicago and is favored by truckers who want to roll without encountering the highway patrol. In a car I never would have thought of 54 as an alternate to the interstates but a bicycle gives you a feel for the flow of roads and why they go where they do. In my mind's eye, I could see Routes 54 and 60 sweeping southwest out of the heartland and 60 meandering west over the Continental Divide and 64 cutting a jagged pattern across the New Mexican outback. They were the arteries that kept alive the Rookie League towns like Nara Visa and fed into the interstates that connected the Triple-A towns to the cities. Like a riverboat captain on the Mississippi, I knew—or thought I did—every bend in my chosen route and understood where obstacles lay and how to find safe passage. In a car, I just went, sometimes not even knowing the precise direction of my travel; on a bicycle each jog of the road is distinct and the route stays with you not as a montage of snapshots but as a continuous, moving thing that picks its course as does a mountain stream.

The hills and winds slowed my pace to Logan, which I had figured I would reach by early afternoon but did not get to until dark. Trucks shot through town at sixty-five miles an hour without so much as a hiss of their brakes. I watched the road from a booth in a café, looking for two yellow rain slickers, but Norma and Evie did not show up and I went ahead and ordered dinner. I hoped they had not encountered trouble. I supposed they were out there, somewhere in the darkness, working hard to get to Logan.

Tucumcari—the Comanche name for a nearby 700-foot peak from which they sent signals—is an AA town, a morning's ride, or about twenty-five miles, from Logan. It straddles what was U.S. 66, now marked, where it survives, as Historic 66, a state route. Unpaved until 1937, the road was designated a military highway in World War II, with civilian traffic limited to thirty-five miles an hour. I had come into Tucumcari one night thirty-five years earlier, a teenager hitchhiking from the East Coast to California, and remember the explosion of neon lights from motels and restaurants along 66 that lit up the sky. It was a grand sight on a lonely highway. Now Interstate 40 dodges around Tucumcari's perimeter and the westbound Greyhound out of St. Louis pauses only long enough for a fast coffee break, but the town holds firm, pretending it is still an important overnight stop on the road west. The town is strung out for a couple of miles along a wide boulevard and I biked the length of it, turning into motel courtyards, cruising through truck stops, circling the town hall and post office. Tucumcari has a good feel, like something out of the fifties when the open road sang of more romance than it does today. Some of the motels I passed—the Apache, Pony Soldier, Blue Swallow, Pow Wow and Palomino—had stood guard over the old highway since the days of radio and Wurlitzer jukeboxes. At night Tucumcari still blazes with neon lights and in a piano bar I heard an entertainer from Albuquerque sing Bobby Troup's "(Get Your Kicks on) Route 66" ("If you ever plan to motor west . . . take the highway that's best. . . ."). It's a bouncy tune but somehow it sounded melancholy to me, because in an era when travelers drive right through the night, seeing nothing but a high-speed lane, Tucumcari, though a fine road town, really doesn't matter anymore.

4

IF YOU FIND TUCUMCARI ON A MAP OF NEW MEXICO, you'll see that I had gotten myself into something of a pickle. Here was the problem: Riding a bicycle on New Mexico's interstates is prohibited, but of the three routes out of Tucumcari, the only sensible way was on I-40 west, which leads straight to the doorstep of Los Angeles. If I took 104 north into the Sangre de Cristo Mountains, I'd dead-end at another interstate, I-25, and solve nothing. If I took 209 south to Ragland, I'd have to make my way over gravel roads to Route 60 and that road, too, would eventually dump me onto I-25. Either way, north or south, would cost me days and a hundred or more miles and not get me where I wanted to go. The irony was that interstates in the rural West are safer for cyclists than the two-lane roads I'd been on. The untraveled shoulder is a full lane wide and the ramps—which represent the only real danger when an exiting motorist misjudges the speed of a biker ahead continuing straight—are infrequent and miles apart. A simple solution would be to require bikers to leave the interstate at each off-ramp and permit them to return to it on the on-ramp. I called the state department of transportation to politely inquire how in hell I was meant to get across New Mexico without using the interstate.

The call caused some confusion and it was a few minutes before I was connected to a knowledgeable official. He didn't know how much of the old 66 was navigable as a frontage road but confirmed the interstate ban (unless I had a special permit, which was not available on short notice), though he said some highway patrolmen enforced the prohibition, others didn't. It depended on their mood. West of Albuquerque, he said, was usually no problem; east of Albuquerque a particular lieutenant delighted in making life miserable for the occasional biker who happened through. I asked what would happen if I were stopped. "They might just tell you to get off at the next exit or they might drive you back to Tucumcari and make you start over, on another road," the official said, and went on to recount the story of a biker who broke down in tears when dropped off on a road he'd left three days earlier. I would have cried, too. I followed the 66 frontage road until it turned into broken pavement a few miles from Tucumcari, then lugged my bike over a grassy strip and paused at the entrance ramp to I-40. The sign there said, NO CYCLISTS OR PEDESTRIANS ALLOWED. I pedaled by it and in a minute was flying down the interstate at a good clip, the morning air filled with the whoosh of cars and eighteen-wheelers barreling westward.

Gandhi said, "There is more to life than increasing its speed," and any traveler who knows the pleasure of wandering our old historic highways would certainly concur. The interstates have stolen from us the chance of discovery, yet this much I must admit: After so long in the solitude of the America that lives on a two-lane blacktop, Interstate 40 brought sheer elation. It was as though I had come down off a mountain and rejoined the world. Being among fellow travelers again was reassuring. I liked seeing signs that told me what restaurants and motels lay ahead and how many miles I had to go to reach them. The shoulder was wide and smooth. Passing motorists and truckers greeted me with two quick taps on the horn. I responded with a thumbs-up wave.

In the days before interstates, the federal government took the first steps in creating a national highway system by improving the existing network of two-lane roads, such as U.S. 66, for military and civilian traffic. But in 1939, after a four-year survey revealed increasing congestion and roads that did not meet defense needs, the Bureau of Public Roads announced long-range plans to develop a nationwide network of superhighways, linking forty-one state capitals and almost every city with a population of fifty thousand or more. A secondary system of feeder roads would reach out to rural-free-delivery and public-school-bus routes. Cars,

the bureau reasoned, needed their own high-speed transportation corridors, just as railroads did, and from its proposal
eventually evolved, in 1956, the National System of Interstate
and Defense Highways that would change the way we traveled. The interstate system was financed largely through a
state and federal gasoline tax (every penny of tax on a gallon
of gas raises an additional $1 billion). Every mile that was con-
structed in the 45,000-mile network ate up forty-five acres.

If what we cared about in the fifties was speed and ease of
travel, it is worth noting that the nineties brought a major
philosophical change in mapping the future of transportation.
Under the Intermodal Surface Transportation Efficiency Act
of 1991, or ISTEA (pronounced "ice tea")—the federal blue
print that replaced the interstate act—less emphasis is placed
on building new highways and more on repairing existing
roads and providing alternatives to the single-occupant vehicle. Among them is the bicycle. The $155 billion, six-year
ISTEA program mandates that each state's transportation department appoint a bicycle and pedestrian coordinator and
that every state and metropolitan area have a long-range bi
cycle plan. The act gives local governments flexibility in de-
signing systems compatible with community needs and
encourages schemes that incorporate biking, walking and
public transit with the automobile. For the first time under a
federal program, funds are as readily available for the construction of bike-parking facilities and bike paths as they were
forty years ago for the building of eight-lane highways. It
seems odd that after believing bigger and faster was better for
so long, we should now be looking at something that is sim-
pler and slower as an integral part of our transportation future,
on short-haul commutes at least.

One of the most imaginative programs ISTEA helps fund is the conversion of rails to trails, an idea that may result in bicyclists—and joggers, walkers and Rollerbladers—being able one day to travel coast-to-coast through a scenic corridor of narrow, off-road parks. With railroads merging, consolidating routes, sometimes going out of business and taking advantage of deregulation that enables them to abandon unprofitable lines, 160,000 miles of railbed (a figure that grows by 3,000 miles a year) now lie idle throughout the country. But they are not yet lost. The Rails-to-Trails Conservancy, a nonprofit organization in Washington, D.C., has overseen the transformation of 7,039 miles of abandoned railbeds into wide, manicured trails. Bikers in all forty-eight contiguous states now have access to former rail lines—Wisconsin has the most extensive system with 756 miles, Kansas and Arizona the smallest, with 1 mile each—and the conservancy hopes to have 10,000 miles in place by the turn of the century. Its long-range goal is to reconnect America with a network of trails that would span the continent and keep folks like me off the interstates forever.

I had been on I-40 for about ten miles when a white Toyota pickup pulled onto the shoulder ahead and stopped. "Are you David Lamb?" the driver asked. After being a stranger everywhere I had traveled for six weeks, the sound of my own name startled me. The driver, who had a muddied mountain bike in the back of his truck, introduced himself as Jeff Penna. He was a former actor from New York who had moved to Santa Fe and founded the American Bicycle and Cycling Museum. "Isn't it strange," he said, "that we have national museums for everything in this country—even oysters—but not one for the bicycle that's been around for a hundred twenty years?" A few days earlier, he had tracked me down on the phone after reading one of my travelogue articles in the *Los Angeles Times* and said he'd enjoy talking about my trip over coffee or a drink. We set up an imprecise meeting point: If he was in the area the following Thursday, he'd find me somewhere west of Tucumcari. I followed his pickup to Stuckey's at the next exit ramp.

Jeff was active in a citizens' advocacy group that was lobbying state officials to be more accommodating to cyclists—a potential source of substantial tourist revenue—and to lift the interstate prohibition. Among other things, he said, this would allow bikers to explore what remains of the Santa Fe Trail, which runs along I-25. We talked over coffee at Stuckey's for an hour, with me spending a good part of the time fretting about the likelihood of getting stopped and tossed off the interstate. "I don't know what your ground rules are," he said, "but from here I'm going to Albuquerque and I'll be glad to give you and your bike a lift. I could drop you at the frontage road in Moriarty that'll take you to Albuquerque and you won't have to worry about being hassled by the patrol."

"I don't have any rules," I said. "Let's do it."

Perhaps I should have felt like a charlatan but no guilt gnawed at me. I settled into the passenger seat and watched the high-country plains roll by, but my eye was still that of a biker, not a motorist. The direction of the thunderheads above, the bending clumps of grass that meant the wind was picking up, the smoothness of the road were all things I contemplated, though they no longer had any impact on my progress while I sat on an upholstered seat with a rolled-up window. Jeff was a fine guide, full of knowledge and curiosity about the land and the state, and we turned off the interstate to examine the dying remains of Montoya and Newkirk and Cuervo, which had once been living, breathing towns on the old 66. By the time he left me in Moriarty we had covered a hundred miles, turning what would have been a two-day bike trip into a two-hour car hop. Albuquerque was thirty miles away on a road that ran downhill and I flew into town and turned down Edith Boulevard just ahead of a lightning storm, at 40 mph, fast enough to get a speeding ticket. I made my way to the home of friends who had lived in Egypt when Sandy and I did. I walked my bike into their garage and by habit started to lift it over the threshold to their kitchen. They gave me a strange look and I caught myself, remembering that in the normal world one does not set his bicycle up next to the bed.

5

AN EARLY WINTER STORM STRUCK THE HIGH COUNTRY overnight, closing the road ahead, from Gallup, New Mexico, to Flagstaff, Arizona, under a foot of heavy, wet snow. Autumn was gone in a flash. In the mountains the only reminder of October were the cottonwoods, their fiery yellow leaves tossing in the winds of a world turned white. I decided to make my way to Grants, seventy-eight miles from Albuquerque, to wait out the storm before venturing into the Rockies. The road was rain-puddled. It rose out of the mile-high valley around Albuquerque, snaked through the mesas of the Cañoncito, Laguna and Acoma Indian Reservations, and, at an elevation of 6,400 feet, brought me into Grants, an old mining town named for two brothers who had set up a camp for railroad workers in the 1880s. To the west the Rockies reached across the horizon like a sky-high barricade of stone, snow-covered and cloud-shrouded. Six weeks earlier the sight of them would have unnerved me. Now the notion they might defeat me never crossed my mind. I had only to use my wits and, if necessary, bide my time. The snow would melt. Or I could hitch a ride with a trailer truck. Or I could buy bicycle chains at the local bicycle shop. Getting up and over was but the prelude to what lay on the far side of the Continental Divide—a road headed down to the Pacific, altitude zero. I went looking for a warm place with cable TV tuned to The Weather Channel.

Grants is a funny place. It still has sixteen motels and thirty restaurants, a throwback to the days when U.S. 66 went straight through town. It sits on the world's largest uranium deposits, discovered in 1950, which for a generation made Grants a boom town. Then, in the early eighties, the interstate came through and the recession hit. Sixty-six emptied, the mines closed. In an attempt to give the town a boost, Grants recently built a multimillion-dollar golf course but wasn't doing well attracting golfers from Albuquerque or anywhere else. I checked out the town. It was Sunday afternoon. Most of the men I saw on the street were drunk. The women were tattooed. The bars buzzed with hard drinkers, chasing shots of whiskey with beer. They had the dull-eyed look of men just out of the mines. The problem was that the last shift had gone home ten years ago.

I met a salesman who was sober in one of the taverns. He had retired from the U.S. Army as a major, not a high rank to achieve after twenty years' service. "I know I wasn't on the fast track," he said, "but basically I achieved my goals—to serve my country and see a little of the world." The television at the end of the bar was tuned to The Weather Channel. He, too, was waiting for the storm to lift and had come off the interstate for the night en route to Gallup. Three weeks a month he was on the road, selling restaurant supplies, and though he liked the freedom of the job and the people he met, he missed the military. "In terms of integration, equality of pay, getting promoted on your merits, the military's the model of what the rest of our society ought to be. I always felt I was doing something worthwhile in the Army because you don't do it just to get a paycheck or to make yourself a general. You're part of a team, a family, really, and I liked that. It gives you what kids today haven't ever learned: discipline, self-sacrifice, respect. All the things that make the group more valuable than the individual. The only thing that bugs me about my career is that I never saw combat. I was too young for Vietnam and I was in Korea when the Persian Gulf war broke out. It's not that I'm bloodthirsty or anything, but I think everyone wonders how he'd react under fire, whether he'd let his buddies down or rise to the occasion. I think I would have handled it okay but I'll never know for sure."

In a way he was talking about the test of self that comes with risk taking, and though introspection has never been my strong suit, part of my motivation in making this journey was, no doubt, simply to see how I'd react to the challenge of risk. The risk of failure. The risk of loneliness. The risk of injury or mishap. For me middle age, and the awareness of one's vulnerability that comes with it, have not been conducive to increased risk taking. I took chances as a twenty-eight-year-old reporter in Vietnam that I would not have taken as a fifty-one-year-old reporter in the Persian Gulf war. My instincts in Vietnam told me, "Hell, nothing can happen to me"; in Saudi Arabia they said, "Play it smart and get out alive." Middle age also brings, for me anyway, an acceptance of one's limitations. One morning you awake and realize you're not going to be Hemingway or the president of the company, that the torch has been passed to a new generation that works cheaper and maybe smarter. These people travel the fast track you once moved on, and to prove—to yourself or others?—that you're still capable of extraordinary deeds, you do something your friends consider foolhardy, like riding your bicycle across America. But as one travels, the words of Joseph Addison, the eighteenth-century English essayist, might well provide a useful reminder: "Men may change their climate, but they cannot change their nature. A man that goes out a fool cannot ride or sail himself into common sense."

Thick clouds still clung to the Rockies in the morning but the forecast was for clearing skies and warming temperatures. It was time to take my chances in the mountains and I pedaled out of Grants on the old 66 toward Milan, Bluewater and Prewitt, my map of little help because it showed only I-40 but not the wandering path of the frontage road. The Santa Fe tracks run parallel to the two-lane highway and on them, heading west and east, a constant stream of mile-long freight trains, piggybacking trailer upon trailer, hightailed it for distant railyards. The raw wind raced me through the mountain passes, snow-covered buttes to my right and left, and all about me a Western landscape as wide and handsome as anything I had ever seen. The road was swept clear of snow by giant plows and gentler temperatures and rose so gradually toward the Continental Divide that I was unaware of climbing. I moved easily along the rooftop of North America, not even having to shift into a low gear, the intimidation I had felt at the thought of crossing the Rockies having melted as quickly as the snow. A great distance ahead, I watched an eastbound Santa Fe freight come rumbling toward me. The tracks were no more than fifty yards from the empty road and as we passed, the engineer leaned from his window and waved, saluting with three long blasts of his whistle that rolled across the silent plain. Seldom have I felt more alone or more important.

Just past the town of Thoreau (pronounced "throw") I slipped over the Continental Divide, at 7,766 feet above sea level, suffering neither a shortage of breath nor any tinges of fatigue. Ha! My editor at the *Times* had lost ten dollars betting I wouldn't even make the Divide. Had I been carrying champagne I would have popped a cork, but I had only raisins and cigarettes to commemorate the moment, so I set my bike on its kickstand and sat on a stretch of roadside gravel, atop a mountain chain, 65 million years old, that reaches three thousand miles from Canada to Mexico. The temperature was thirty-eight degrees, though it did not feel that cold. For the first time in three days the sun broke through a few patches in the cloud layer.

Route 66—numbered Route 122 in some places—is a good, though unpredictable, road. Sometimes it runs for miles, well maintained and smooth, then suddenly gives way to broken pavement and gravel. Smack-dab in the middle of the road will be a diamond-shaped yellow sign warning ROAD

CLOSED. Other times 66 dips and climbs and twists like a Slinky while the interstate next to it flows flat and straight. I shot by a gas station and from the corner of my eye caught sight of two people in yellow rain slickers by the air pump. *Hey!* I did a U-turn in the empty road and went back. Sure enough, it was my road mates, Norma Witherbee and Evie Weber. Seeing them was like finding a friend long lost and we swapped tales of flat tires and steady progress and tried to figure out why we had not stumbled into one another in Tucumcari, Albuquerque or Grants. They, too, had used I-40, after Special Olympics had wrangled them an interstate permit upon posting a $1 million bond. The insurance company initially balked, saying it doubted two women riding alone across the country without even a support van were safe at any price. "Nonsense," replied Evie. "We've biked everywhere and never had any trouble."

The three of us traveled together for a ways, drafting and making good time, and agreed to meet for dinner at a motel in Gallup that I had found listed in the yellow pages. I pulled ahead and rode for two hours, not stopping until I happened on the Giant Travel Center, "the largest truck stop in USA," so big it had its own interstate exit ramp. Hundreds of semis stretched across the parking lot, in bumper-to-bumper formation, engines rumbling like an armada of tanks going to war, shiny Peterbilts and cab-over Macks and big-nosed Internationals, each forty tons of rubber and steel, chromed radiator grilles polished, doors painted with the names of far-off towns, some of the rigs veterans of a million road miles.

> *There'd be no truckdrivers if it wasn't for us trucks*
> *No double-clutching gearjamming coffee-drinking nuts*

They drive their way to glory
And they have all the luck
There'd be no truckdrivers if it wasn't for us trucks.

The restaurant was half the size of a football field. All the booths were equipped with phones for making credit-card calls and I settled into one, with a copy of *USA Today*. I checked the date by the masthead to see if today was Monday or Tuesday, not that it mattered. Coffee came by the thermos, my coconut pie with three inches of cream topping. I no longer wore a watch and was surprised when I left that the clock on the wall read five. Darkness was setting in and the temperature was dropping back toward freezing. I hammered out the final seventeen miles of the day in an hour, turning off the interstate and doubling back over a bridge that leads into Gallup. Like Tucumcari, Gallup is huddled along Historic 66. It has a large community of Native Americans and the highest incidence of alcoholism of any town in the country. The glow of splashy neon signs lit up the storefronts. The rambling old motels were filling up. I half expected to see fin-tailed Caddies and vintage Corvettes cruising the street and to hear the voice of Nat "King" Cole coming from a three-plays-for-a-quarter jukebox. WHERE THE MOVIE STARS STAY, said the El Rancho Motel sign, though I doubted that Gallup saw many movie stars these days. Evie and Norma arrived a couple of hours after I did, well past sunset. Evie's brake cable had snapped and she had walked her bike the last mile into Gallup, Norma following just behind. That could have ended their California journey right there, but Evie was undaunted. She carried a spare cable. She called a friend in Chicago, who talked her through sizing and cutting the cable, threading it into a passageway on the handlebars, fastening it to the anchor bolts and adjusting tension so the pivot bolts pulled properly. She turned the bike back upright, clinched the brake levers and said, with a note of triumph, "We did it. They feel perfect. We're ready to roll tomorrow." I don't think I ever said as much to the ladies from Chicago, but I owed them a debt of gratitude for teaching me a great deal about attitude and self-reliance.

6

BICYCLES ARE AMONG THE COMMON DENOMINATORS OF our lives. We all grew up on one. The bicycle brought us our first taste of freedom. It taught us about the dangers inherent to the road (we rode facing oncoming traffic in those days) and the purpose of gears and brakes and ball bearings. The first thing we probably ever repaired was a flat tire. And, at least for those of us who have been around a while, the first meaningful possession we junked was our bicycle, discarded as a symbol of adolescence the day we turned old enough to drive a car. It's safe to assume that if I had shown up at college with a bicycle in 1958, I would have immediately been dismissed as a twit and had no more luck finding a Saturday night date than I would have a bike shop. But, like wide ties and crew cuts, the bicycle is back, enjoying an adult renaissance reminiscent of the cycling craze that swept Europe and the United States a century ago.

Though you couldn't prove it by the number of bicycles I'd seen crossing the country—was it six, including my own?—the Bicycle Federation of America, a nonprofit organization in Washington, D.C., that promotes the increased use of bicycles for all purposes, estimates there are 55 million adult cyclists in the United States, including 31 million who bike regularly. More than 3 million Americans commute to work at least occasionally on a bicycle and over 1 million Americans take biking vacations every year. Annual bicycle sales have grown to 13 million—Californians buy one of every six—and the number of bikes in the country to 120 million, just about equaling the number of cars. Globally, 100 million bicycles are manufactured a year and the number of bikes in the world is nearing 1 billion. The Chinese alone buy more bicycles a year (35 million) than the rest of the world does cars.

Though the bicycle is the prime source of transportation for the majority of the world's people, transportation experts not long ago were predicting that the manufacture of automobiles would overtake that of bicycles as developing countries built roads and incomes rose. In 1969 the annual production gap had narrowed to 25 million bicycles and 23 million cars. But global production of bicycles has been surging since 1970, widening the gap to the point where today bicycles outsell cars almost three to one. One obvious explanation is economics: 80 percent of the world's people can afford a bicycle (though it may be a serious investment for many); less than 10 percent can afford a car.

It is difficult to pinpoint the precise reasons, or even the date, of the bicycle's return to fashion in the Western world. Certainly the fitness movement and concerns about the environment played a big role, as did the oil crises of 1973 and 1979, when commuters began looking for alternate forms of transportation. Some people in the $3-billion-a-year U.S. bicycle industry trace the roots of the United States bike boom back to the late 1960s when John Lindsay, the mayor of New York City, appointed a wealthy, young freethinker with no experience in urban recreation as his parks commissioner. The first thing Thomas Hoving did was to take a look at the six miles of congested roads in Central Park and say, "Let's close down the park to cars on weekends." What a nutty idea, the critics howled, but almost overnight bicycle rental businesses appeared near the park and within weeks thousands of adults who hadn't been on a bike in years were wheeling their way along the park's carless roads. The idea spread. Rental shops flourished from California to Florida, bikes and biking gear got spiffier, and before long adults who wanted a bicycle weren't limited to what Sears, Roebuck and the local department stores had on the rack. They shopped instead at one of the five thousand independent dealers whose shops sprung up around the country, offering, as strange as it would have seemed a few years earlier, only a single product: bicycles.

In the Western world, we usually bicycle by choice, not necessity, but in much of the underdeveloped world where cars are both unaffordable and a symbol of progress, a stigma remains attached to the bicycle: It is the technology of the poor. Better to sweep it off the streets as a sign of backwardness than to design transportation systems for it, the reasoning goes. In Kenya, British colonial authorities wrote a comprehensive plan for Nairobi in the 1940s that included an extensive network of bicycle pathways for commuting and getting goods to market; the independent government that came to power in 1963 never acted on the plan, building roads for cars instead, and by 1990, with traffic congestion growing and nary a bicyclist in sight, 41 percent of Nairobi's workers were getting to work on foot. The oil-rich emirate of Abu Dhabi banned bicycling on city streets entirely in 1981, allegedly to reduce the number of traffic accidents. The World Bank published a 400-page study of China's transportation sector in 1988 without once mentioning bicycles, of which the country has 300 million. In Indonesia, between 1989 and 1994, Jakarta confiscated and dumped into the sea more than 100,000 cycle rickshaws, ostensibly to reduce congestion.

José Antonio Viera-Gallo, Chile's assistant secretary of justice under Salvador Allende, may have overstated his case when he said, "Socialism can only be achieved on a bicycle," but undeniably the bicycle has proved itself the most affordable, egalitarian, utilitarian, speedy and reliable short-haul people-mover the masses have ever had access to. Far more than a plaything, as we view it in the United States, the bicycle is of the future, a vehicle that has a role in the transportation systems of a world transformed by the automobile. For some European countries that never abandoned a tradition of cycling, this is hardly news.

In Denmark, the Netherlands and Germany, for instance, bike owners outnumber non-owners. Half of the 300,000 commuters who use the Netherlands' national railway system to get to work travel between their homes and the rail stations by bicycle. The Dutch government spent $230 million between 1975 and 1985 to construct cycleways and parking, and to increase transit access through bicycle facilities at rail stations. By the early 1980s, Dutch expenditures on bicycle projects exceeded capital spending on roadways. In Denmark, where poets have celebrated the bicycle and sculptors have made statues of cyclists, one survey reports that 32 percent of workers commute by bicycle to their jobs and another 9 percent pedal to the train station. More than 75 percent of Denmark's roads include bike lanes. The Netherlands' and Denmark's bike-friendly environments have turned "bicycle tourism" into a major industry, with thousands of foreign visitors pedaling off through country towns on extended vacations.

"What sets apart the handful of countries that, in a world seduced by automobiles, have chosen to embrace the bicycle?" asks Marcia D. Lowe in her report on global bicycle use for Worldwatch Institute. "These few cycling societies are not notably different, in terms of living standards, geography or climate, from their noncycling neighbors. A study by John Purcher, a professor of urban planning at Rutgers University, of 'urban travel behavior' in twelve North American and Western European countries confirms that wide variations in people's transport decisions are not chiefly influenced by levels of income, technology or urbanization. The difference lies in enlightened public policy and strong government support."

7

THERE ARE SO MANY THINGS THAT CAN MESS UP A POTENtially good bicycling day: wind, hills, weather, traffic, bad roads. Maybe only one day in fifteen had I encountered what I'd call perfect conditions, and on those windless-flat-cool-uncongested-smooth-rolling days life was very good indeed. "For my part," Robert Louis Stevenson once wrote, "I travel not to go anywhere, but to go. I travel for travel's sake. The great affair is to move," and on those good days I knew exactly what he meant. I had not grown bored with the steady movement of my life, though I doubt I could have enjoyed it as much if I had no chosen destination. Unlike Stevenson, I needed to know where I was going and when the journey would end. This discovery rather surprised me because I had always thought I could be content aimlessly wandering the country eight or ten months a year, in an RV or even by train or bus. Now I asked myself, "If the road does not lead home, what can be the purpose?" Though my progress sometimes seemed achingly slow when judged by the accomplishments of a single day, the road itself—its towns and dreary motels and look-alike cafés—never became monotonous because there was always the anticipation of rounding an unfamiliar bend and saying, as had Brigham Young when he led his Mormons west and gazed upon the valley at the base of Utah's Wasatch and Oquirrh ranges, "*This* is the place!"

The thermometer was stuck at twenty-two degrees the morning I left Gallup. I dressed in layers, leggings over shorts, mittens over biking gloves, windbreaker and sweater over short-sleeve jersey, so I could shed my clothes piece by piece as the temperature rose. The aspens had been stripped of autumn's last leaves and the alpine meadows were spotted with patches of snow. I tried the frontage road for three miles but it was hilly and rough and I got a flat and, at the first opportunity, I pedaled back onto I-40. All the world was in motion again: snowbirds heading to Arizona for the winter in motor homes and Airstreams, truckers bound for Amarillo and Jacksonville, Phoenix and San Bernardino, uprooted families hauling U-Haul trailers, the 7:45 A.M. Greyhound out of St. Louis bearing a destination marker that said LOS ANGELES. No longer the interloper that I had been in the early stages of my journey, I felt a natural part of the highway flow. This was my road as much as theirs. The vistas were expansive and grand wherever I looked, broken only by exit-ramp billboards for mom-and-pop Navajo enterprises that weren't much more than pit stops for tourists: INDIAN CITY DON'T MISS IT, one sign said. INDIAN RUINS, ALL JEWELRY 70% OFF, said another, and SEE FORT COURAGE, HOME OF F TROOP (wasn't that a TV show?). Usually I stopped as directed, but the run-down little businesses struck me as a sad legacy of the Navajo nation and I never stayed long.

I crossed the New Mexico–Arizona border near Lupton and pulled into a line of trailer trucks at the state agricultural inspection station. The silvery trailer to my front was four or five times taller and perhaps ten times wider than was I seated on my narrow frame; the red-nosed International behind me hissed and strained like a reined-in horse as we inched forward. Talk about an ant in a field of elephants. "Are you carrying any produce?" the inspection man asked, all business despite the foolishness of his question. "A box of raisins and some Fig Newtons are about all that would qualify," I said. He waved me through. I found a comfortable gear and moseyed on.

Riding a bicycle on the interstate is legal in Arizona, except on the congested stretch of I-10 between Tucson and Phoenix, and it was a relief not to have butterflies take wing in my stomach every time I passed a highway patrolman. My good fortune was short-lived, for in a few miles I made an un-happy discovery about Arizona's interstates: The shoulder lane is grooved to jar awake sleepy drivers drifting off the road. The grooves are cut several inches deep into the pave-ment and placed every four feet, diagonally across the width of the lane: *kaa-bump, kaa-bump, kaa-bump.* They were too close together to swerve around and I rattled over them as though some invisible force were picking me up and drop-ping me every few feet. I could imagine my spokes buckling, my tires going flat, my rims collapsing. I loosened my grip on the handlebar and tried to relax my arms and legs so they would become shock absorbers. To the list of things that can foul up a good day, add grooves.

In a truck stop café I asked the waitress if the grooves went all the way to California. "We have people asking about weather, speed traps, that sort of thing, but nobody's ever asked about grooves before," she said. "Tell you the truth, I don't think I ever noticed them." Despite the grooves, not much stood between me and the Pacific now. I matched up my Arizona and California maps and, anchoring their seam with a coffee cup and pie plate, spread them across the table. For the first time I allowed myself to place my thumb and forefinger two inches apart—a distance that represented sev-enty-five miles on my map, or a day's travel—and pace off the approximate time it would take to get to Santa Monica. About two weeks looked right, figuring in a writing day in Arizona and a gambling day in Nevada.

"Excuse me, my partner and I were looking at your bike," a tall young truck driver in cowboy clothes said, coming up to my table. "Do you mind me asking where you're coming from?" His civility reminded me, again, how inherent politeness is to the character of the American heartland, where strangers approach with apologies for the possibility they might be intruding. "Join me?" I asked, but he said he and his partner couldn't dawdle: They had bought the rig parked across the road six months ago and "we have to keep it running night and day to make the payments." He was white, his partner black. It was the only example of intimate contact between two races I saw on the trip, though it was common to see blacks and whites and Native Americans working and talking together and moving, apparently comfortably, through the peripheries of one another's world. But unlike the two truckers now standing at my table, most of us have never taken the time to get to know one another, and in those soils of ignorance, our stereotypes take firm root. The man in the Stetson appeared to be in his late twenties and was lean as a bean stalk. He said his parents used to own a bike shop and he had often dreamed of seeing the country by bicycle, but he knew he never would. I asked why.

"I wouldn't have the spirit to make it," he said.

The remark stayed with me for miles. "I wouldn't have the spirit." How could he know this? How could someone young and fit believe his mind, not his body, would fail him? And not having tried to bike cross-country, how was he wise enough to know that mental discipline was a bigger challenge than physical endurance? I wasn't sure if I were more heartened that he had marked me as a someone with "spirit" or more saddened that someone so young had already placed limitations on what he was capable of doing.

I used alternate routes for the next several days, sticking to the interstate when I found ungrooved stretches and cutting back onto 66 when it was passable and some little town along its cracked pavement caught my eye. The motels in Chambers and Holbrook—the one in Chambers had set aside one of its rooms as the town post office—were empty when I checked in. Then at dusk motorists poured off the highway like rats abandoning the ship and within thirty or forty minutes every room had been taken. By breakfast time the next morning, everyone had moved on and the motels were again deserted. It was a strange spectacle to see my world fill and empty as if on cue every day, to realize most people didn't even know what town they had chosen for their home that night. After holing up in Holbrook an extra day to write an article for the *Los Angeles Times* and to phone Voice of America ("Aren't you making better time than you'd planned on?" the VOA interviewer asked), I wheeled my bike out of the room to get an early-morning start on the ninety-three-mile run to Flagstaff. Outside my door, a man and his wife were in their new Ford, suitcases piled in the backseat. I could see him bend forward to turn the ignition key. The engine whined but did not catch. He tried it again and again and each time got only a chorus of coughs and sputters in response. I balanced on my left pedal, kicked off with my right foot and was on my way, for Jackrabbit, Apache Butte, Two Guns and Winona, the whine of the man's unwilling engine soon fading.

The VOA interviewer was right. I was making good time, primarily, I think, because I unwittingly had found a corollary between my past experience writing books and my attempt to cross the country on a bicycle: The process of completing each activity is identical. You start from a position of intimidation, not a word written or a mile logged. The initial journey is rough and uncertain and filled with the prospect of failure. Then, almost without warning, you awake one morning to learn you are headed where you want to go and a rhythm sets in that carries you from one day to the next. The farther you go, the more obsessed you become with the destination, and as improbable as reaching it once seemed, you understand that if you do this thing faithfully— writing six hundred or seven hundred words a day, biking fifty or sixty miles, or whatever—you eventually will get there. But you must do it every day, particularly when you have lost the will to proceed. Writer's block or ennui cannot be permitted to slow your progress. Perhaps that's what the young trucker meant when he talked about "spirit."

It's a good distance between cafés on the road from Holbrook to Flagstaff. My hunger grew. For twenty miles I followed the billboards that counted down the miles to a truck stop in Twin Arrows, on Historic 66, and could all but smell coffee perking and hamburgers cooking by the time I pedaled into the dirt parking lot of the café, a twisting mile off the interstate. Half a dozen trailer trucks were parked out back. I hoped there would be homemade pie and a booth where I could stretch out. I tried the door. It was locked. A handwritten sign in the window said, SORRY WE ARE CLOSED. THANKS FOR STOPPING. MERRY CHRISTMAS. I wondered if the owner had ever considered taking down his interstate billboards. I circled the trucks, whose drivers were slumped in the front seats, asleep, and headed for Flagstaff, thirty miles off, on a road cut straight through the mountain cliffs. The final twelve miles into Flagstaff are all uphill and I wasn't surprised at all when I made out the forms of two bicyclists ahead, pushing determinedly up the long, steep road. It was the sisters from Chicago and we rode together into town.

8

IN THE LATE 1920S *ARIZONA HIGHWAYS* MAGAZINE DE-
scribed Route 66 between Flagstaff and Williams as a "narrow, crooked, poorly surfaced road which is particularly
dangerous in dry weather due to ravelling and innumerable
potholes." In those days—when the federal government
capped road-building expenditures at $10,000 a mile (com-
pared with the $19 million it costs today to construct the av-
erage mile of roadway)—engineers yielded to the influence of
the landscape. Their roads, like mountain streams, followed
the path of least resistance, picking their way around hills,
through valleys and along riverbeds, twisting over escarp-
ments without the benefit of cuts and fills to improve align-
ment. They coexisted with the landscape, rather than
dominating it, as would interstates. The first surveys for what
would become America's most famous road west were con-
ducted in the 1850s by Edward Beale, a former U.S. Navy
lieutenant, appointed by the secretary of war to construct a
wagon road across Arizona, from Fort Defiance to the mouth
of the Mojave River. Using camels imported from Arabia and
Egypt as pack animals, he found a way roughly along the
thirty-fifth parallel that followed centuries-old Indian trails.
Over the years Beale's road became known by many names—
the National Old Trails Highway, the Santa Fe Highway, the
Postal Highway, the Grand Canyon Route, the Will Rogers

Highway—but only one name stuck to become part of our travel mythology: Route 66.

Coming out of Flagstaff, I saw, for the first time, a sign with my destination on it: LOS ANGELES 482 MILES. Interstate 40 lies atop the old 66 between Flagstaff and Williams and I sped along its smooth, ungrooved shoulder, the sky crystal blue, the air crisp. I was on a high plateau, among ponderosa pines, and on either side of me and ahead of me an unpopulated land of stark beauty reached for miles, through canyons and buttes and rain-gorged ravines. "Hello out there!" I shouted, and I heard my voice echo back. I was as close as I will ever come to knowing the freedom of the cowboy and the pure exhilaration of aloneness and independence. I thought back to the journey's beginnings, in Virginia, and could not imagine that my knees had ever been full of pain or that I had almost quit. What a fool I would have been, and, not knowing what awaited me, I would not even have realized I had been a fool.

Williams is named for Bill Williams, a trapper and guide killed by Indians in 1849, and I arrived there just as the daily train from the Grand Canyon pulled into town, pillars of thick, white steam rushing from the smokestack of the ancient locomotive. The engineer gave three long pulls on a cord in his cab and the whistle responded with a screamlike wail that rolled over the town and slid down my spine. It was a sight and a sound I could never tire of. "We've heard that whistle every day at five o'clock long as I can remember. I can remember hearing it as a little girl," said the woman at the bar who, like me, had stopped at Rod's Steak House for a drink. The restaurant, once known to virtually every over-the-road driver between Chicago and Los Angeles, carries the name of

Rod Graves, who was born in Maine in 1904, dropped out of Stanford and ended up owning a great Arizona ranch under the MJ Bar brand. He built the restaurant at the end of World War II, saying travelers should be able to eat as good a steak on Route 66 as he could at his ranch, and ran it until 1967, when he dropped dead the day after selling out. The restaurant is now owned by Lawrence Sanchez, Rod's former dishwasher.

My beer came. "Listen now, the whistle's going to blow one more time," the woman next to me said. It did. The woman did not look like a road person. Her hair was coiffured and she wore alligator cowboy boots and a buckskin suit and a lot of Indian jewelry that, I suspect, was expensive. Perfumed, powdered and elegant in a cowgirlish way, she could have been forty-five or sixty-five. She had been born in Williams, she said, the daughter of a railroad worker, and had gone to school, and for a while lived, in a railroad car operated by the company for employee families. She had run the Monte Carlo Truck Stop and Bar outside Williams during the heyday of Route 66 and sold out about the time Rod Graves did, to move to Phoenix. I asked if she liked it there and she said, "Phoenix's been good to me. You have to go where the money is." An edition of that day's newspaper was folded on the bar in front of her. It bore a page-one story on the shooting death of a truck driver who had pulled off I-25 near Santa Fe to sleep. The robbery had netted the killer less than five dollars. An accompanying photograph showed a young man, in handcuffs, being led into court for arraignment. He was smiling.

"Now, may I ask you what made you take *this* journey *this* time of year, *alone*?" she said. "You're not safe alone anymore. There are too many nuts out there. You break down and they offer to help and they'll kill you instead. On top of that, they'll throw your body over the railing. A woman like me alone can't be too careful. I carry a .44 revolver, Smith and Wesson, long barrel, and I keep it right on the dash where people can see it. I've got a CB radio and a nine-band police radio, two-way, so if there's a highway patrolman within fifty miles of me, I can reach him. It didn't used to be like that but you don't know who you can trust anymore."

She was cagey about what business she was in, though I gathered she bought and sold Indian jewelry. It had been many years, she said, since she had been in Williams and what had brought her back was simply a curiosity to see how the town had fared with the death of U.S. 66 and who was left and what had happened to the three-room cottage her father had owned. She had spent the day looking for old friends.

"So was it worth the trip?" I asked.

"Not really. I come back and everybody's dead. It's like coming home to a ghost town."

Oklahoma has more surviving miles (400) of U.S. 66 than any other state, but the longest uninterrupted section you can still drive or bike (158 miles) is in Arizona. It starts in Seligman (population 850), a day's ride from Williams, and winds through Peach Springs, Truxton, Valentine, Kingman and Oatman to Topock on the California border. Angel Delgadillo, the barber in Seligman, is president of Arizona's Historic Route 66 Association, a grassroots group that promotes the old highway as a tourist attraction—"Do yourself a favor. Get off the interstate and come see America," he is fond of saying—and in the process has saved the little towns along the way from certain death. I stopped at the barbershop. It was unlocked but no one was inside and I assumed Angel had gone to lunch. So I biked down the road to the Copper Cart to get a sandwich and read the paper. The weekly *Independent Voice* ("I am the voice of today, the herald of tomorrow") noted that the local high school football team had been beaten the previous week, trailing Ash Fork 48–6 at the half. It said the Antelopes had played hard "but were inconsistent on defense." Half of Angel's barbershop has been turned into a museum of Route 66 memorabilia and when I returned, a young man from Switzerland, his wife, son and parents in tow, was browsing through a stack of recent articles about the highway in magazines from Brazil, France, Germany, Great Britain, Spain. He and his family had planned their vacation for two years and were spending all their time in the United States tracking what remains of U.S. 66, from Chicago to Los Angeles. He said his only regret was that he had been unable to rent a 1950s convertible from Hertz. I asked what in the world someone from Europe would find so compelling about a broken-down, two-lane highway that hardly anyone lived on.

"America, cars, the open road—this is what we think of when we talk of America," he said. "Your history is here. Going west. The Dust Bowl. Small towns. Restless energy. This is the image of America I've always had, being able to do exactly what we're doing now. Being on 66 is like watching a documentary. I just wish I could have rented a convertible."

It was a romantic view and one I did not quibble with. Though Route 66 has become an almost generic term for road life before the interstates—and thus lives on the nostalgia for days that were slower, more innocent and not without trust—the highway is a symbol of a nation's westward experience and it does warrant a communal nod of recognition. I had traveled it from Seligman to Kingman three times before—in a car, in an RV and as a hitchhiker—and could remember many of its bends, its abandoned roundhouses and shuttered Harvey House restaurants run by the railroad, its closed one-room schoolhouses and Mobil gas signs of a flying red horse, blowing idly in the wind. But on a bicycle 66 looks different, does not feel like a ghost road. Instead of seeing what was dead, I was cognizant of what was alive—the towns themselves that, after all, had not given up, the hardy desert flowers and the cacti that held secret stocks of water, the breeze and sunshine and smell of cattle in the autumn air.

Ray Barker, the founder of the Historic Route 66 Association, and his wife, Mildred, ran the Frontier Motel and Café in Truxton, and they had been gracious when I had last come through, seven or eight years earlier, sharing their tales of a lifetime spent on Route 66, in Sayre, Oklahoma, Grants, New Mexico, and now Truxton, Arizona. I leaned my bike against the café sign and went in. Ray's mother was on a walker now, making her way to a booth, and his eighty-eight-year-old stepfather was seated at the counter, talking to no one in particular about busting broncos and being born in the Cherokee Nation before Oklahoma was even a state. Mildred came out of the kitchen, luncheon plates in each hand, and recognized me. "You still in that RV?" she asked. No, I said, I had found something slower and cheaper this time, and nodded outside. "My word," she said.

I asked if Ray were about. "Ray passed on four years ago,"

she said. "My daughter's come back to help out and we only keep the café open from seven to seven now, but it's an awful lot of work. I'm really undecided what to do. I think about leaving, but then I get to remembering the effort Ray put into keeping this road alive, and I'm not sure I could just turn my back on all that. You get old and staying put's a lot easier than moving on, you know."

Mildred made me a hamburger special, with French fries and coleslaw, and a milk shake, and I stuck around talking longer than I should have. It was 3:30 P.M. when I got up to leave and, because northern Arizona doesn't observe daylight saving time, preferring instead an extra hour of cooler nighttime temperatures, I had little more than two hours of light left if I wanted to make the forty miles to Kingman before dark. I looked outside to see if someone was driving a pickup that I might be able to catch a ride with. There was only my bike and a battered VW Beetle in the gravel parking lot.

"I'm going to treat you today to lunch," Mildred said.

"Please," I said, "you're working hard enough as it is without giving out free lunches. Let me pay."

"I insist."

I pedaled out of the parking lot and turned left toward Hackberry and Kingman on Historic Route 66, thinking how many people like Mildred Barker—and before her, Ray—I had met along our two-lane roads. They worked hard and long and honest. It was the only way they knew how to live.

9

*I have no home. My home is where my extra luggage is,
and where the car is stored, and where I happen to be getting mail this time. My home is America.*

—ERNIE PYLE

LONG BEFORE BECOMING FAMOUS AS A WAR CORRESPON-
dent, Ernie Pyle was America's best-known travel writer, a
sort of Charles Kuralt of the 1930s who wandered the country in a Ford Coupe, searching out stories of everyday life that
other journalists ignored. Though a Midwesterner by birth
and an Easterner by necessity of work, Pyle found his greatest
joy in the West, captivated by a sense of openness in both its
land and its people. "Each time, after leaving," he wrote in a
column for Scripps-Howard newspapers, "I realize that in the
West my spirit has been light; I've felt freer and happier." And
in a letter to a friend in 1937 he said: "Am I glad to get West
again! The three months in the East damn near killed me. . . .
When I crossed the Mississippi River I felt as though I'd shed
a big burden." Pyle would have made a fine biking companion, and if he were around today, I suspect he'd find that re-
gional distinctiveness still exists in the United States and that
the West's character remains unique. It's not just the breadth
of the prairies and mountains or the size of the sky that is special, it is the *feel* of the place. I, too, had been "freer and happier" these last few days than at any time since leaving home,
eight weeks and 2,600 miles ago. Around each curve I found
a landscape exactly as my grandfather would have seen it,

going west from Duluth by train a century ago. In the little towns—where the saloon was always older than the post office or church—dreams floated back from my Boston youth, when I used to thumb through magazines looking for pictures of Randolph Scott and anything reminiscent of the Old West. On the thin two-lane roads Conestoga wagons pulled by plodding oxen came into focus and Jack Kerouac raced by ("A fast car, a coast to reach and a woman at the end of the road" is all that matters) and John Steinbeck poked along with Charley, on his final, sad journey, to reacquaint himself with an America he had lost touch with.

The open road is more about the past than the present, more about who we were than who we are. That, I suppose, is what pulls me and so many others back to it. It speaks of nostalgia for our mythic past, of westering and all that the frontier connotes. For some, movement on it is an end in itself; and for the mavericks among that restless lot, the bicycle and the road are a perfect fit.

After traveling roads devoid of bikers for so long, I suddenly started running into them all over the place on 66. One was pedaling out of a motel parking lot in Ash Fork, a young man headed from Richmond to Los Angeles. He had gotten separated from his friend, somewhere around Williams, but figured they'd find each other within a day or two. We biked together half a mile to the end of town, swapping quick stories, before I turned back to get breakfast and a haircut at the Bull Pen truck stop. Later, while I was fixing a flat on a stretch of highway where only two cars had passed me in thirty minutes, an eastbound biker approached. He was a retired Colorado high school teacher, on his first cycling tour, tracking the old U.S. 66 from Los Angeles to

Albuquerque. His wife, keeping her own pace in a camper trailer, rendezvoused with him periodically throughout the day and cooked the meals. He had planned his trip so that he would be back home for Election Day, and when I said I originally thought I'd be on the road until Thanksgiving, he replied: "But how were you going to *vote*?" Then there was the German lad, big-bellied, shirtless in forty-degree temperatures, the color of a groundhog, laboring up a long ascent on a three-speed bike loaded with enough pots, pans, camping gear and American mementos to stock a department store. I asked him when he figured to make Chicago, knowing the weather was getting dicey in the Rockies. "Chicago?" he said. "No, I am going to the Grand Canyon, then Mexico and Guatemala, maybe Panama." Every time I thought I was hot stuff someone came along to quietly remind me of my place. Everyone I met mentioned seeing other bikers in the past couple of days. One said he'd talked to two women from Chicago and I was glad to know Evie and Norma were well. Another referred to two young men, westbound, on mountain bikes, and I said, "That must be the guys from Richmond who got separated." It was as though I knew all the important travelers on 66 for a hundred miles in either direction.

In Kingman, after a night in a truck-stop motel, I stopped to peer into the "air-cooled" Beale Hotel, where Clark Gable and Carole Lombard spent the first night of their honeymoon in 1939, and to consult my map. The road gave me four choices: I-40 dipped south to Yucca, 66 meandered on to Goldroad and Oatman, 93 shot northwest to Las Vegas and 68 went straight west, up over Union Pass and the Mojave Mountains, to Bullhead City on the Colorado River. I went straight. I passed the perimeters of desert communities so new they weren't even on my map: cinder-block house after cinder-block house lining treeless street after treeless street, reaching out to the foothills, a collection of anonymous Levittowns advertised on billboards as "ranch estates." They were Phoenix, circa 1950.

The climb over Union Pass was tough and I paused at the summit, 3,265 feet high, the sprawling developments gone from sight now, canyon walls all about and in the distance, the tops of mountains that belonged to Nevada and California. The ten-mile descent to the Colorado River on the Arizona–Nevada border was so steep I kept my hands on the brake levers and did not dare go flat-out. I sped through a landscape of stone and desert, without vegetation, the earth a sunbaked brown. The road banked sharply left and in the valley below, on the riverbank, lay Bullhead City, which is not a city at all but merely a tired town of desert monochrome and two-story buildings. On the far side of the Colorado, the Nevada side, the gambling town of Laughlin appeared as a mirage. It was in Technicolor: Expansive emerald-green lawns stretched back from the shore, corridors of red and yellow flowers lined the walkways, brand-new hotel-casinos, outlined in neon, with balconies and swimming pools, soared thirty stories over the river. Construction cranes reached across the skyline. Coming into Laughlin was like crossing the Sinai and, upon leaving the Arab lands, entering Israel. The desert had been transformed.

All the casinos run ferry shuttles across the narrow river, between Arizona and Nevada, and when the Hilton's docked, I started to push my bike aboard. The captain waved me off. "No bicycles allowed," he said. "Try the Riverside. I think they'll take you." I biked half a mile up the river and got onto the Riverside's ferry without attracting a second glance. In the hotel the receptionist didn't seem to think anything was askew either when I checked in hauling a bicycle instead of luggage. She rented me a deluxe seventh-floor room for twenty-four dollars, and I made my way through the packed casino to the elevators, steering my bike down alleyways of slot machines, extending "excuse me's" as my saddlebags bumped the stools of elderly overweight women hunched over machines alive with the clanking of coins, and turned left by the row of blackjack tables. To the best of my knowledge, not a single head turned from the piles of chips and buckets of quarters to look in my direction.

The Riverside is owned by Laughlin's founder, Don Laughlin (Nevada must be the only state where you can still name a town for yourself), who settled in the Colorado River Valley thirty years ago when there wasn't anything around except a boarded-up eight-room motel and empty desert. Laughlin had grown up in Owatonna, Minnesota, and as an enterprising teenager had turned a single slot machine he bought in a mail-order catalog into a booming business. By the time he was sixteen he had slots in all the town's taverns and, even after splitting profits with the owners, was netting five hundred dollars a week. The high school principal said he had to get out of the slot business or get out of school. The choice was a no-brainer, Laughlin said, and he quit school. He moved to Las Vegas, went to dealer's school, learned how to repair slot machines, worked as a bartender and for ten years, until 1964, ran a North Las Vegas joint called the 101 Club. A couple of years later, he bought the shuttered motel in then nameless Laughlin for $35,000 down.

He put his family in four of the rooms, rented out the other four and, to attract gamblers to the twelve slot machines and two gaming tables he had set up, started offering all-you-can-eat chicken dinners for ninety-eight cents. From my balcony, where my bike was parked, I could see Don Laughlin's helicopter on the pad below. Staff and security agents and associates lined up as though paying homage to a head of state whenever he lifted off for his 1,500-acre ranch near Kingman. His payroll at the Riverside had reached $32 million and plans were under way for a 1,500-room, twenty-eight-story hotel extension. To promote the town, Don Laughlin had done what the county could not, spending $3.5 million for a bridge across the Colorado and $9 million for flood control and the design of an airport, which opened in 1991. His reward: Laughlin now generates the third-highest gambling revenues in Nevada, after Las Vegas and Reno.

Laughlin offered an excellent reprieve from the road and I awoke at the Riverside to a day with absolutely nothing to do. My journal was up-to-date, my laundry had been done in the RV park across the road, my bike was in good working order for the push to the Pacific. I had no stories to write, no miles to ride. I went to a movie after breakfast in the hotel's theater—it's a wonderfully wicked experience to watch a first-run film at eight-thirty on a Tuesday morning—and to a magic show in another casino before lunch. I ate, drank, shot some craps and napped. I walked around town and watched security officers patrolling the casino parking lots on mountain bikes. Then I got restless. I went back up to my room and again checked my tire pressure and studied my maps. I bet a couple of horses in the bookie parlor downstairs—finishing out of the money in one race and losing a

photo finish in another—and I paced around idly, waiting for
the arrival of Mike Kennedy, my friend from Los Angeles,
who was going to join me on the final four- or five-day ride
to Santa Monica.

10

OF ALL THE FRIENDS/ACQUAINTANCES/QUASI-STRANGERS
who asked if they could bike part of the way across the
United States with me—apprehensive of incompatibility, I
usually said no—Mike Kennedy was the surest bet. Mike had
been at the *Los Angeles Times* nearly as long as I, but I hadn't
known him well until we both ended up in Beirut in 1982
to cover the fifth Arab-Israeli war. Being there that summer
was like waiting for your own funeral. Gangs of wild-eyed
loonies roved the streets, shooting anything they felt like
killing, the Israelis shelled us day after day from hilltop posi-
tions overlooking the Mediterranean, car bombs brought
down buildings, and assassinations, massacres and banditry
built up fears you couldn't shake loose. With escape routes
from the besieged city sealed off by Israel and the warring
militias, Mike and I were seldom out of each other's sight for
three months: We ate our meals together, ran around the
same danger zones together, and hung out together for last
call at the Commodore Hotel bar. It was as close as two
straight guys could come to being married.

So when Mike offered to join me crossing the Mojave, I knew I'd be in good company. He'd rented a car in Los Angeles and pulled into Laughlin at 8 P.M., carrying his disassembled bike in the backseat and a fifth of Dickel Bourbon in his saddlebags. I had figured we'd carouse the casinos half the night and probably head off in the morning with banging hangovers, but damn, my staying powers had ebbed to shameful levels over the years, and I didn't make it much beyond dinner before my eyes grew heavy. We left Laughlin clearheaded the next morning, following a winding road down the Colorado River to Needles, California. For nearly two months I had dreamed of crossing into California, dreamed of reaching this El Dorado where the grass is greener and the water sweeter, and now I slipped over a border marked by a sign that said I was entering San Bernardino County but made no mention of California. Ahead, as behind, lay white-rocked cliffs and scorching, vacant desert.

"Wait till we get to California," Steinbeck's Pa Joad said when the Joad family crossed the border not far from here, down to its last forty dollars, during the Dust Bowl exodus. "You'll see nice country then."

"Jesus Christ, Pa!" Tom Joad replied. "This here *is* California."

Needles—or Needless Needles, as the locals call it—is an old Sante Fe railroad town on Historic 66 living on borrowed time. Unlike Seligman and the Arizona towns I had seen that had survived because of sheer obstinacy and the Route 66 nostalgia industry, Needles had been baked into lethargy by the desert sun. Downtown stores were abandoned, pavement was crumbling on glass-littered streets, the grand old train depot was boarded up. The town raises $600,000 a year through a 10 percent room tax on motels, but the Chamber of Commerce gets only $7,000 of that for promotion, much of the rest going to pay down loans on a new money-losing municipal golf course. I looked for signs to remind me that history had passed through Needles on the old 66, but couldn't find any. "When I moved into town and bought this place," said the motel owner where Mike and I shared a room, "I had all the business community over for lunch one day. It was a fine time. Then I mentioned that perhaps we could do something to put Needles back on the map, like fixing the roads, sprucing up downtown. That really turned them off. They thought I was an agitator, an outsider who had no right to criticize. I was almost run out of town. I still say hello when I see them but we don't really talk anymore."

Mike and I filled the water bottles on our bikes for the ride across the desert, and stuck four extra quart bottles and a bagful of candy bars in our saddlebags. Mike, no novice to bicycle touring, was a companion of boundless good cheer. I could hear him behind me on the road, humming tunes and carrying on one-way conversations that I could not quite make out. It was, I decided, the normal response of a man who finds himself snatched from the office on a weekday morning and set down on a big, beautiful Western road going nowhere and everywhere. In the glaring sun, the sharp outline of our shadows followed us on the pavement. A few miles out of Needles, the road starts a twenty-seven-mile ascent over the Dead Mountains. Mike—younger by nine years, I should point out—pulled ahead. At the Mountain Springs Summit, 2,300 feet above Needles, we caught up with another biker, sweat-drenched, huffing hard, also pointed toward Los Angeles. His name was Richard, and dressed in fatigues, boots and a baseball cap, riding a one-speed girl's bike, he made for an odd sight. He carried no water and we offered him one of our bottles, which he drained in no time.

"You guys know how far to Laughlin?" he asked. "It can't be much farther."

He said he had gotten drunk, put his car in a ditch in Needles and it had been impounded. He intended to win enough money at the tables in Laughlin to get it back. California dreamin' at its purest. He asked for more water and dropped the container I handed him. I thought for a minute he might be suffering sunstroke, then it dawned on me: Richard was flat-out *shit-faced*. He was on an interstate, in the middle of the desert with no water or food, on a clanky old bike that would have been difficult to pedal on the flats, much less over a mountain, going in the wrong direction, and he was shit-faced!

"Richard," Mike said, "Laughlin's east. Back down the mountain." Richard blinked. A four-hour climb had been for naught. "Well," he said, with logic that defied comment, "at least the next stretch is downhill." Not questioning our directions for a moment, he hauled his bike across the center divider and we watched Wrong-way Richard pedal off, this time eastbound, gaining speed on the descent, the blackjack tables still a long day's ride away.

The Mojave ranks with the Oklahoma Panhandle in terms of arduous biking—in the hundred miles from Needles to Ludlow there is not a gas station, not a café, not a house, not a sign of life except the highway itself—and I was thankful to be making the run with a friend. Bicyclists crossing the Mojave in summer travel by night to avoid temperatures in the 130s; even now, in late October, the daytime mercury topped

90 degrees and the only shade we could find was under an occasional bridge that carries a road over I-40. We'd stop at each to rest and gulp water.

"I am in the middle of the dreariest, deadest-looking country imaginable," Thomas Stevens said of the Western desert during his cross-country bicycle journey in 1884. "Whirlwinds of sand, looking at a distance like huge columns of smoke, are wandering erratically over the plains in all directions. The blazing sun casts, with startling vividness on the smooth white alkali, that awful scraggy, straggling shadow that, like a vengeful fate, always accompanies the cycler on a sunny day, and which is the bane of a sensitive wheelman's life!"

Mike was a stronger biker than I. Refreshed by the shade, we'd set out together, pedaling at what seemed to be the same cadence, and in ten or twelve minutes, he'd be a couple of miles ahead. My energy level had peaked. My body did what was asked of it but no longer willingly gave more than it had to. Burnout—the weariness that comes with repetition—was setting in. My legs moved out of force of habit. Our supply of water had turned hot and our candy, except for the M&M's, had melted. I could taste the sand in my mouth. Our odometers passed sixty miles for the day, then seventy, eighty. Darkness came. Joshua trees became semaphores in the shadows of the desert and the distant mountains turned dark blue. At six o'clock, stiff headwinds hitting us straight on hour after hour, progress slow, Ludlow was still twenty-six miles distant. Suddenly, without warning, the wind turned and was at our backs. "Allll rrright!" Mike yelled. We flew, kitelike, down the highway, carried by the wind, and within an hour the lights of Ludlow flickered in the darkness ahead. We turned off I-40, the sand glowing in the moonlight like snow, and biked into a town consisting of two gas stations, a small motel, several homes tucked back into the rocks and one darned good café that makes double-thick milk shakes. A note taped to the door of the motel office said, PLEASE INQUIRE AT CHEVRON STATION. There was one room left—the last available room between Ludlow and Barstow, fifty miles off, it turned out—and we took it. No Ritz-Carlton ever looked more welcoming.

"Watch out for the weirdos," a railroad man had said in Needles. "The desert's full of 'em. We got some here, but nothing like they got in Barstow." It was true: The desert is a strange place and I do not understand the people who live there by choice, other than knowing they are in flight from civilization. In the desert, as nowhere else, Americans can live without rules or regulations and when they tire of the place, they simply pick up and leave. Down the road, near Barstow and farther west, over the next two days we passed clusters of humble homes that looked as though they would not withstand a stiff gale. Their yards—like those I had seen in Alaskan Eskimo villages—were filled with discarded washing machines, old tires, skeletons of automobiles and all manner of odd parts, broken-down equipment and junk. IF ANYTHING IN THIS YARD IS WORTH YOUR LIFE, BE MY GUEST, warned the sign outside one man's house. The land, unforgiving, inhospitable, was breathtaking in its sense of timeless beauty. It made you feel small. Yet what man had put on it was unsightly and did not feel permanent. I was a stranger here among the sand dunes and creosote bush, in a desert larger than West Virginia, and knew I did not belong.

Mike and I alternated between I-40—which is illegal for

bicyclists to ride in California, but not a black-and-white patrol car passed us for a hundred miles—and, where it existed, Route 66. We stopped for lunch in Newberry Springs at the Sidewinder Café—the filming location for the cult movie *Bagdad Café*—and stumbled onto isolated towns like Daggett that seemed imported from West Texas, with railroad tracks running down the wide deserted National Old Trails Highway and a row of squat, one-story, adobe-colored shops and homes that appeared uninhabited. Following our route was like thumbing through an old *Saturday Evening Post.* "I moved here from North Carolina, twenty-four years ago," a woman in Palmdale said, "and my kids are grown up, still back there. They keep saying, 'Mom, come on home,' and I say, 'What's there? Why go back?' Sure, times are tough right now. Military bases in the desert are closing down, the aerospace industry is pulling out. On my street there are ten homes for sale, and I'd say half those ten owners walked away. Just locked the door and walked away. To hell with the mortgage and all. But California will come back. It has everything to offer. It's still where you come when you've got dreams."

We had hoped to make Palmdale the third day out of Needles, but we came up twenty miles short, set back by disagreeable headwinds, and we sought refuge at nightfall in Pearblossom's six-room motel, on the western edge of the desert. The motel owner, glad to have company, drove the half mile into town and brought back a six-pack, which the three of us drank in his office/home. No traffic moved on Route 138 and the world around us felt as vast and empty as the Arctic. Yet—and I had a hard time comprehending this—we were now in Los Angeles County. Twenty-two million people lived within a day's drive. The desert was being prepped for Los Angeles's expansion. The county had bought up surrounding water rights and topped the wells, waiting for the people who would come to the Antelope Valley when Los Angeles could hold no more. Fire hydrants had been placed in barren stretches of sand, streets had been imagined and named, their signs implanted in the desert where not a house stood for thousands of yards in any direction: 123 ST E, E AVE V–8, E AVE V–10.

By bicycle, Los Angeles looked to be an easy two-days' ride from Pearblossom. Daylight saving time ended that night and we left at sunup, which now came at 7 A.M., crossing through the San Gabriel Mountains on a low road that hugged the Soledad Canyon, along a riverbed, and pointed us downhill though everything on either side headed up. The road was swift and smooth, the Mojave's way, I thought, of saying, "Here's a thank-you for sticking with me for so long." Mike had decided it was fitting for me to make the last day's ride to the Santa Monica Pier alone and planned to turn off for home when we got to Northridge. I concurred, but was glad the journey's end was at hand and I did not have much furthur to pedal on alone. Having left my cocoon, I had rediscovered the pleasure of talking with a friend about familiar things. We came out of the canyon, turned a corner, and the America I had lived in for two months was gone. Ahead, in the basin below, spread the San Fernando Valley, earthquake-shattered, freeway-laced, people-packed. The traffic became heavy and no one waved or moved aside for me anymore. Bicyclists were everywhere, dressed in the latest multicolored polyester outfits for their Sunday-morning ride, their lean, clean cherry bikes burdened by not a single saddlebag or bedroll. None gave the dusty, tattered road warrior in their midst a second glance. I felt like a combat veteran in an arena of draft dodgers. I stopped in a fancy deli with potted plants hanging from the ceiling and ordered a baloney sandwich, extra mayo, on white. "*White* bread?" the man said. "Sure you want white? How 'bout alfalfa sprouts?" I ate the sandwich at a table—white bread, no sprouts—and lit a cigarette with my coffee. "No smoking!" the man barked, annoyed now. "You'll have to go outside to do that."

I was back, back in the Other America.

11

I DON'T WANT TO MAKE TOO MUCH OF THIS BICYCLING thing. The bicycle is not the salvation of a polluted, congested planet, as some of its activist advocates would have us believe. It's not a very practical way to cross the United States, unless time is of no consequence, and it has some disadvantages as a vehicle for doing errands at home if being rained on, honked at and weighted down with packages sours your disposition. But with our cities car-clogged and traffic slowing to a crawl—by the year 2000 the average Los Angeles resident will spend five to seven a hours a week stalled in traffic jams, the U.S. government says—there are a few considerations worth noting:

•If 10 percent of the nation's car commuters switched to bicycles—or a combination of bicycles and public transit—

our annual fuel bill for imported oil would drop by more than $1 billion.

•Bicycling to work would save the average car commuter 400 gallons of gasoline a year. Using a bike just to get to the bus or rail station would save 150 gallons.

•Building a downtown parking structure can cost $30,000 per car space; a bike locker costs $200. Put another way, eighteen bicycles can park in the space used by one car.

•In traffic, thirty bicycles can move through the highway area devoured by one car. They emit no pollutants, use no fuel, cause no traffic jams.

•It takes two lanes of a given size, writes Ivan Illich, in *Energy and Equity,* to move forty thousand people across a bridge in one hour using modern trains. By bus, it takes four lanes; by car, twelve. Forty thousand bicyclists need only one.

Americans drive 2.2 trillion miles a year, the equivalent of eighty-eight times around the globe. We spend $70 billion annually on transportation infrastructure, yet we're falling behind: Our bridges need repair, and so do our highways. Our airports are outdated, our railbeds as antiquated as Zaire's. New York City collects $800 million a year from fuel taxes, tolls and other transportation fees and still can't match what it spends to maintain its crumbling roads. Traditionally federal and state governments have had a simple response to the crisis caused by our dependence on the automobile: Build more roads. "We cannot solve the problems that we have created," Albert Einstein once said, speaking of something other than traffic congestion, "with the same thinking that created them," yet few of us, myself included, could imagine life without the freedom to pack up our cars any darn time we want and discover where the road goes.

Ever since New York built the nation's first bike path, on Ocean Parkway in Brooklyn, in 1895, people have been looking for ways to incorporate the bicycle into our transportation system. Robert Moses, the city planner, proposed a network of bike lanes in New York City in the 1930s, and New York City Mayor Ed Koch was so taken with the bicycle's usefulness during a trip to China in 1980 that he came home and hastily had barriers erected to create two six-foot-wide bike lanes between Greenwich Village and Central Park. Koch showed up for the opening ceremony in a limousine. The experiment did not fare well. Motorists ignored the lanes, several pedestrians in them were severely injured by bicyclists, and despite a burst of initial enthusiasm, bikers traveled them less and less. Koch soured on the idea within a year after seeing only two cyclists using the lanes on a weekend day—one of them going the wrong way—and ordered the cement blocks defining the lanes removed. "I was swept away by the thought of what could be when I saw a million bikes in Beijing," he said. "And I see two in New York City—on a Sunday. . . . My own gut tells me the lanes aren't working."

Unlike Japan, where a quarter of all daily passenger trips in Tokyo are by bicycle, or Denmark, where a third of the adult population bikes to work, bicycles have not made the transition in the United States from recreational vehicle to utilitarian transporter because most people perceive them as offering an unsafe, inconvenient way to get around. It is the vehicle of last resort, its use demarcated by economic means: Of those who bike to work in the United States, there are twice as many commuters with incomes under $15,000 a year as there are commuters earning over $35,000. But a Harris Poll, commissioned by *Bicycling* magazine in 1991, said that the number of occasional and regular bike commuters would rise tenfold, to over 35 million, if "bike-friendly" transportation systems existed—safe bike lanes, facilities to park and lock bikes, showers at the work site, city buses with bike racks to integrate biking and public transport. Others have reached similar conclusions. When, for instance, Madison, Wisconsin, built one of the country's most sophisticated networks of bike paths, linking the suburbs with downtown, the share of bicycle traffic on Madison's streets jumped from 4 percent to 11 percent.

Half of all car trips in the United States are under five miles, so the likelihood that the bicycle could play a significant role in the transportation systems of the twenty-first century may not be as pie-in-the-sky as it sounds. The Intermodal Surface Transportation Efficiency Act—the federal blueprint for lessening our dependence on single-occupant cars by making biking, walking and public transit easier—already is nudging us toward alternate means of getting from here to there. Southern California's air-quality program mandates that all companies with a hundred or more employees implement plans to get workers out of their cars and onto bicycles or into public transport. And in city after city, the bicycle is carving out a niche in the future's transportation system.

More than six hundred municipalities now have police officers patrolling the streets and parks on bikes. "On a bike," said officer Linda Erwin of the Alexandria, Virginia, police department, "you tend to roll right up on stuff happening, like drug deals." In Portland, Oregon, a community group has borrowed an idea from Holland and placed a hundred lemon-yellow, secondhand bicycles on busy downtown sidewalks. Anyone can ride away for free and drop the bike off at some other location. Flat tires have been a problem, but not theft. To reduce the dominance of the automobile, Santa Monica gives city workers who regularly bicycle to work an extra dollar a day in pay; Pasadena employees get free bike maintenance. Los Angeles is spending $50 million on programs to make the city more bike friendly, and in Davis, California—like Madison, a college town—an extensive network of interlinking bike paths has increased the bicyclists' share of all daily trips to 25 percent, the highest in the nation. At Fleetwood Enterprises, of Riverside, California, the world's largest maker of recreational vehicles and trailer homes, 10 percent of the company's 650-person labor force commutes to work by bike. Their reward: free helmets, reflective vests, headlights and mirrors provided by Fleetwood, as well as shower and parking facilities, discounts at a local bike shop, a work area with tools to fix flats and make repairs and a guaranteed ride home—by car—for family emergencies. Company executives celebrated the first anniversary of the "Blood, Sweat and Gears" program by cooking a free breakfast for the bike commuters.

From my vantage point above the San Fernando Valley, I could see eight lanes of traffic moving as in a single convoy along the Foothill Freeway. A blanket of smog blocked the sunlight. I wasn't kidding myself, though. I wasn't going to return home and give up my car. I wasn't going to come back to Los Angeles in twenty years and find everyone on bicycles. The bicycle is not the solution to the crises posed by our romance with the automobile. But it's part of the solution.

12

Only that traveling is good which reveals to me the value of home, and enables me to enjoy it better.
—HENRY DAVID THOREAU

THE MESSAGE SANDY PUT ON OUR HOME ANSWERING MACHINE Sunday night said: "If you're calling for an update on the great bicycle adventure, Dave's in California, closing in on the Pacific. He figures he'll get to the Santa Monica Pier tomorrow, Monday—Halloween Day—between 2 and 3 P.M." I listened to the recording, then hit the Number 2 key on the phone to replay it, as though needing confirmation that it was me who had schlepped alone over the Appalachians and Ozarks, across the Oklahoma Panhandle, through the high desert of Arizona and into the Los Angeles basin. In a way, I suppose, I was still a bit of a fraud because the whole undertaking had been out of character for me. I am not one who has to scale a mountain "because it's there," nor have I ever understood the mystery of what compels men to cross Antarctica by dogsled or circle the world in a balloon. Whatever foolhardy escapades I have taken on, the purpose has been to merely stay afloat. The explanation is as simple as that. I don't care about winning the race. I just want to keep moving, and not always with the current, so that the journey doesn't repeat itself. It is how I keep my balance.

With only twenty-five miles to ride the final day, I didn't bother to fill my water bottles or give my bike its daily check for deflated tires, wobbly spokes, loosened chain. I dallied over breakfast and started late, with just one hill left to climb—up over the 1,380-foot-high Sepulveda Pass that cyclists call the Wall. My appearance had taken on a road-tattered look—the jersey faded and worn from too many hand-scrubbings in motel sinks, the gray shorts torn and shapeless as a burlap bag—but I was feeling really fine. My city pallor had disappeared, along with eight pounds, unused muscles were no longer dormant and, although I didn't know it at the time, my cholesterol level had dropped from a you're-almost-dead 270 to a you're-healthy-as-hell 225. Had I followed my doctor's advice I'd have been a nonsmoking, nondrinking zombie working on a lifetime prescription of cholesterol pills and I wouldn't have had any fun at all these past two months. His advice was perfectly sound medically, I'm sure; it's just that he neglected to offer a commonsense remedy as an alternative: "Why don't you go out and do something strenuous for a while and get healthy?"

The Wall is an overrated challenge. I headed up Sepulveda Boulevard, along the old Butterfield Stage route, on a bike lane, the climb short and steep but not requiring me to downshift into my granny gear, and before I had broken into a sweat I was at the tunnel on the summit, and through the Wall. I no longer was even aware of the weight of my saddlebags. The bicycle was part of my body and pedaling, braking and shifting had become coordinated motions that needed no more thought than placing one foot in front of the other on a sidewalk. I swept down into Los Angeles, paralleling the San Diego Freeway, picked up Beverly Glen, crossed Sunset near the Veterans Cemetery, and turned right on Santa Monica Boulevard. I had lived in Santa Monica after moving to Southern California from Denver in 1970 but something had happened to the upscale town of my memories. On every street I turned down looking for familiar sights were vacant-eyed, raggedy homeless people. They were urinating in alleys, pawing through Dumpsters, sprawled in grassy parks, a babble of incoherent voices and gnarled fingers that reached out for money. "Okay, Jock-o, you want to have at it, we'll see who's the best man," a fatigue-clad madman yelled. He shadowboxed his way into the street ahead of me, then retreated back toward a doughnut shop. I accelerated. The headline that flashed to mind said: "Visitor Crossing USA on Bicycle Mugged, Killed Two Miles Short of Finish Line." After the normalcy of the back roads of America that had been my home, I felt as though I had been plopped down on an alien planet.

For those of us who live in seaboard cities, it is easy to forget—or not know—how decent most of America is. I had been in a land where people looked you in the eye and were as apt to work two jobs as one. While California spent more on its prisons than on its two university systems, I had cut straight through the heart of the America whose voice is unheralded and encountered not a moment's fear or a single incident that could be construed as threatening. I was alone, unarmed, vulnerable. And I felt as secure as I did in my own home. The distrustful, wounded America I read about in the newspapers is not where I had been.

I swung onto Seventh Street, past tall elegant palms standing guard over shabby stucco apartment buildings, and turned down Colorado Boulevard. There ahead—3,012 miles, sixty rainless days and eight flat tires from home—was the Santa Monica Pier, jutting into the Pacific.

"Great joy in camp!" Meriwether Lewis had written 189

years earlier when the Corps of Discovery came within view
of the Pacific, and I felt that same elation. What had seemed
a lifetime of miles had been reduced to a few manageable
yards. Tomorrow mere movement would no longer be the
expression of my purpose or achievements. The old Route 66
ended at the Santa Monica Pier, having carried its travelers
and dreamers as far west as they could go, and I pushed onto
it, past the carousel with hand-painted wooden horses and
over the Palisades Beach, toward the string of cafés and bars
perched above the ocean. In those last few feet I was tempted
to raise my arms into the air, as I had seen triumphant bicyclists do in news photographs, but every time I had practiced
the maneuver I had nearly crashed, so I kept both hands
firmly on the handlebars. I heard a cheer and knew immediately that Sandy had laid a surprise on me by notifying friends
in Los Angeles of my arrival. They had strung a vinyl banner
across the pier that said, in foot-high letters, THE FABULOUS
FOOL FINALLY FINISHES! and had brought a flask of whiskey
and two buckets of champagne on ice. I can't remember a
time when being surrounded by friends was so welcome.
"What was it like?" someone asked, but I really didn't have
an answer. People ask the same question when you come
home from a war and there's not much you can say when you
have no shared frame of reference. How could I explain the
contentment and anxiety that comes with being always alone
and having only yourself to rely on? Or the smugness I felt
knowing that if I had listened to the cautious doubters I never
would have left home in the first place? Tourists on the pier
gathered around the welcoming party and asked me to pose
for pictures, apparently on the premise that everyone in Los
Angeles is a celebrity of one sort or another and they could

figure out who I was later. "Aren't you meant to put your front wheel in the ocean?" one of the tourists asked, and he was right, that's the traditional ending of a coast-to-coast bike trip. But I didn't feel in need of symbolic gestures and we rolled up the banner, my fifteen minutes of Warhol fame over, and I headed back up the pier on my bike to the Sheraton Miramar on Wilshire where a friend, Tom Mankiewicz, had reserved for me a spectacular gift—two nights in a suite, gratis.

"Are you sure I can get in looking like this?" I asked him.

"Absolutely," Tom said. "I just saw Anthony Quinn in the lobby and he was dressed a lot shabbier than you are."

The seafront Miramar had undergone a $40 million face-lift and I wheeled my bike right into the marbled, columned lobby, sidestepping the doorman who seemed intent on blocking my way. I only got a few feet before the shrill voice of a receptionist pierced the foyer: "No bicycles! We have a policy. You'll have to check it in storage." This lady was obviously from Mars. Her remark was as insulting as if I'd been with my wife and Miss Mars had said, "You can't check in with *that* woman."

"Ma'am," I said, "the bicycle is going to my room with me. Everything I've got is in the saddlebags. Besides, I've brought my bike into rooms everywhere I've been in the country. I've even been in *the Plaza* with it and they accommodated me." Granted, I was reaching a little because I was referring to the Plaza Truck Stop in Enid, Oklahoma, not the Plaza hotel in New York City. But my point was made, and she agreed that Roberto, the bellman, could deliver the bike to my room via the service elevator. I took the passenger elevator to the seventh floor and beat Roberto to my room by several minutes. After the mom-and-pop motels I had grown accustomed to, I felt like a pauper suddenly transformed into a pasha, and I rattled around the spacious suite, examining this and that. There were four telephones, two TVs, a terry-cloth bathrobe hanging in the closet, a coffeemaker, a built-in hair drier, little kits for sewing on missing buttons and shining your shoes and a collection of fancy soaps and bottles for bathing, shampooing, moisturizing. I searched the menu for something familiar and didn't get much beyond roast suckling pig with risotto milanese and lombard-style boiled beef brisket and salsa verde. Was that food or a disease? I was out of my element, and though I wouldn't have traded my pampered environment for another motel room with a plugged toilet for a moment, I was aware that the transition from the open road would take time.

So that is where my journey ended, in a $280-a-night hotel suite overlooking the Pacific, my bike parked next to the bed. I was feeling pretty good about everything. I called United Airlines to book passage back to Washington, D.C., and make sure I could get my bike aboard. The flight would take four hours and forty-two minutes. There was no sense of loss that, for now, I was leaving the road behind. I had been on the lam a long time and, nobody's fool, I was wise enough to know when it is time to go home.

Afterword

IT IS AUTUMN NOW, A YEAR AFTER MY JOURNEY'S END, AND life again is as it was. I drive to the office, fly to my assignments for the newspaper and find my days a little faster and fuller than I would choose. The bicycle that carried me to California has been relegated to short-haul recreational use, and that saddens me because I know both it and I are capable of greater purpose and distance. The headwinds that slowed me in the Oklahoma Panhandle are mostly forgotten, as is the aloneness that jarred me in the great expanses of the West. The road from home that my mind has chosen to hold on to is flat and smooth. The wind blows at my back. Traffic is light, the weather good and a warm café is never far away. I remember Dean Station in Tennessee and Mildred Barker's hamburgers on Route 66, even the ride across the Mojave, with fondness. From time to time I think about making another long solo by bicycle. I have the maps detailing a bike route from Maine to Florida, another from Seattle to Boston. I would like to think that one day I will set out to follow these unknown roads, but restlessness, I've learned, takes odd turns and twists and I can't be sure if it will again lead me at 10 mph to some far-off destination.

The other day I received a note from Norma Witherbee and Evie Weber, the sisters from Chicago I met in the Panhandle. They enclosed several pictures they had snapped of me crossing the Continental Divide. "Sorry it's taken a year to get these to you," they wrote. "Can't believe how fast time flies by." Their letter was in a carton of mail that awaited me upon my return from three months' traveling—by jet, economy class—in the Middle East. I had fallen back into the life of a foreign correspondent easily, feeling not at all intimidated by the burdens of schlepping through Saudi Arabia and Lebanon and Syria. But looking at the pictures of me atop the rooftop of New Mexico seemed alien, as though someone else were standing there, on his way across America by bicycle. My life had returned to familiar patterns, if not a routine, and the utter freedom and lack of responsibility I had encountered on the open road is now difficult to comprehend.

I suppose when you strip away some of the dramatic detail I cling to, the most extraordinary aspect of my trip was that it was pretty ordinary. In three thousand miles, nothing truly unusual happened. I just got on my bike and went. The fact is, almost anyone could have done it. Even crossing the Rockies—a thought that had more or less terrified me for months—didn't come close to doing me in. Unlike the Eastern mountains, where the straight, steep blacktop goes up and over, the westward road I followed climbed gradually for hundreds of miles, zigzagging around the toughest gradients, and slipped over the crest of the Continental Divide so uneventfully I might have gone right by the top had there not been a sign. So all the things I dreaded—the Rockies, the rain, my own vulnerability—turned out to be threats that did not exist. And at some point, well west of the Divide, I realized that my apprehension of the unknown was as unfounded as the fear of fear itself.

My bike trip is not mentioned anymore over dinner with

friends and I think of it only occasionally, as when I'm driving on a back road and catch myself checking the flutter of leaves to judge the wind's intensity, or when I pass a lone biker loaded down with saddlebags and want to call out, "Carry on, pedaler. The road gets easier just ahead." Perhaps it's just as well the adventure is no longer the subject of conversation, because people always seemed disappointed when they asked, "Did the journey change your life?" and I'd answer, "Not at all." Oh sure, I'd say, I learned the limits of my endurance and I'd gotten closer to the quiet heart of back-roads America than I had ever been, but my life was the same; I was the same. My fifty-fifth birthday came and went and I still worried that my IRA wasn't growing fast enough, and wondered if I would have time for all the things I wanted to do: return to Vietnam for an extended visit, live in Europe, cross the oceans by freighter, ride all the world's great trains, learn how to navigate a paddle wheeler on the Mississippi, spend a winter in Montana, build a cabin in Vermont, drive the Alaskan Highway from Dawson Creek to Fairbanks, write a novel, meet Joe DiMaggio.

As a teenager, long before I knew bicycles were good for anything except banging around the neighborhood, I remember reading *On the Road* and being baffled by the subtleties and hidden messages critics found in Jack Kerouac's boozy prose. All Kerouac wanted to do, he wrote, was "sneak out into the night and disappear somewhere." That's about all I wanted to do with my coast-to-coast ride, too. I wanted to take a look at America without the pressure of deadlines or itineraries. I wanted to wander and dawdle and see how I held up alone. It wasn't very complex, and perhaps that was the secret I unlocked: Middle age—for me, anyway—

didn't have to be complicated. It was neither a beginning nor an end. It was just the in-between, and what I did with those years wasn't necessarily going to be cathartic or mend my flaws. The die was cast, which was fine with me, and as long as I could travel roads to unfamiliar points, I would never weary of the journey.

ALEXANDRIA, VIRGINIA
NOVEMBER 1995

Route Slip

FOR THE SAKE OF BREVITY AND CLARITY I HAVE OMITTED A FEW
connector roads, but linking these towns with a colored marker
on a map of the United States provides a clear and navigable
route across the country. It goes through nine states and covers
just over three thousand miles. In some cases mileage is approximate because of the sidetracking I did in various towns.

ALEXANDRIA TO:	VIA	SECTOR MILES	TOTAL MILES
Virginia: Fredericksburg	Mt. Vernon Bike Path, Route 1	52	52
Orange, Charlottesville, Waynesboro	Routes 3, 20, 231, 250	97	149
Lexington, Roanoke, Pulaski	Route 11	153	302
Marion, Bristol	Route 11	100	402
Tennessee: Kingsport, Bean Station, Knoxville, Rockwood	Routes 11, 70	178	580
Chattanooga, Haletown, Monteagle	Routes 27, 41, 150	122	702
Winchester, Frankewing, Savannah, Memphis	Route 64	292	994
Arkansas: Newport, Mountain View, Marshall	Routes 77, 63, 14, 66, 65	201	1,195

ROUTE SLIP

ALEXANDRIA TO:	VIA	SECTOR MILES	TOTAL MILES
Harrison, Fayetteville, Huntsville, Siloam Springs	Routes 65, 62, 412	146	1,341
Oklahoma: Pryor, Skiatook, Enid	Routes Scenic 412, 69, 20, 99, 64, 77, 412	234	1575
Woodward, Fort Supply, Slapout, Guymon, Boise City	Routes 412, 3	276	1,851
Texas: Dalhart	Routes 385, 54	49	1,900
New Mexico: Logan, Tucumcari, Albuquerque, Grants, Gallup	I-40, Route 66	364	2,264
Arizona: Chambers, Holbrook, Flagstaff, Williams, Seligman, Kingman	I-40, Historic Route 66	363	2,627
Nevada: Laughlin	Route 68	41	2,668
California: Needles	Unmarked road	35	2,703
Ludlow, Barstow, Victorville, Pearblossom	I-40, Routes 66, 18, 138	230	2,933
San Fernando Valley, Los Angeles, Santa Monica	Soledad Canyon Rd., Sepulveda Blvd., Santa Monica Blvd.	79	3,012

Acknowledgments

I OWE MANY THANKS: To people along the way I will never see again but who made a stranger feel welcome; to Dave and Judy McDowell in Albuquerque and Vinny and Elaine Schodolski in Northridge, California, who put me up and cleaned me up; to John and Maggie Lamb, who took a long detour to find me on a stretch of Oklahoma road; to Tom Mankiewicz, always the generous and loyal friend, and most of all, with love, to Sandy, who said, "Go for it," and always believed I'd make it, even when I had doubts.

Irwin Rosten helped shape the manuscript with an editor's pencil and a caring eye. My editors at Times Books, Peter Osnos and Steve Wasserman, and my literary agent, Carl D. Brandt, helped push me westward, even though they never pedaled a mile with me. Mark Murphy and Mike Kennedy reminded me that old-time reporters still make the best company, and Evie Weber and Norma Witherbee that spirit will carry you a long way.

Roger White at the Smithsonian Institution and Richard Weingraff at the Federal Highway Administration offered invaluable assistance by sharing their vast knowledge of our transportation and road systems. Two books, mentioned in the bibliography, provide excellent accounts of the bicycle's early role in society: *The Complete Book of Bicycling,* by Eugene Sloane, and *A Social History of the Bicycle,* by Robert Smith.

Norty Stewart provided invaluable assistance in mapping my route, and Robert Winning's book, *Bicycling Across America,* offered an excellent route slip, from which I borrowed freely.

Thanks as well to my editors at the *Los Angeles Times*—Shelby Coffey, George Cotliar, Mike Miller and Roger Smith—who have the heart to tolerate, and sometimes even encourage, my eccentricities, and to Stacey Aucoin, Brooks Sido and Gregory Wuenschel at the Bicycle Exchange in Virginia, who got me ready for the journey and never raised their eyebrows when I asked a dumb question. Thanks, too, to Larry Lucchino, Bob Caputo, John and Roma Sherman, Priscilla White, David Shaw, David Oyster, Nick and Nicky Noxon, and the Northrop clan: Mike and Susie, Bob and Betsy, Carl and Michaelanne, Kim and Cort.

And to the Betas at the University of Maine, from so long ago—Kit-Babes, Gerb, La-Pit, Beezie, Brownie-A, Moody, Flyface, Don & Dirty, Great Britain and the others—thanks for teaching me about laughter and friendship. The memories of those days kept me smiling, even going across the Oklahoma Panhandle.

Bibliography

Coello, Dennis. *Touring on Two Wheels*. New York: Lyons & Burford, 1988.

Duncan, David. *Pedaling the Ends of the Earth*. New York: Simon & Schuster, 1985.

Geist, Roland C. *Bicycle People*. Washington, D.C.: Acropolis Books, 1978.

Gunther, John. *Inside U.S.A.* New York: Harper & Brothers, 1947.

Illich, Ivan. *Energy and Equity*. London: Calder & Boyars, 1973.

Jenkins, Mark. *Off the Map*. New York: HarperPerennial, 1993.

Labatut, Jean, and Wheaton J. Lane, eds. *Highways in Our National Life*. Princeton, N.J.: Princeton University Press, 1950.

Leccese, Michael, and Arlene Plevin. *The Bicyclist's Sourcebook*. Rockville, Md.: Woodbine House, 1991.

LeMond, Greg, and Kent Gordis. *Greg LeMond's Complete Book of Bicycling*. New York: G.P. Putnam's Sons, 1987.

Leonard, Irving A. *When Bikehood Was in Flower*. Tuscon, Ariz.: Seven Palms Press, 1983.

Lowe, Marcia D. "The Bicycle: Vehicle for a Small Planet." *Worldwatch Paper 90*. Washington, D.C.: Worldwatch Institute, September 1989.

McGurn, James. *On Your Bicycle*. New York: Facts on File, 1987.

Mason, Philip P. *A History of American Roads*. Chicago: Rand McNally & Co., 1967.

Nichols, David, ed. *Ernie's America: The Best of Ernie Pyle's 1930s Travel Dispatches*. New York: Random House, 1989.

Nye, Peter. *The Cyclist's Sourcebook*. New York: Perigee Books, 1991.

———. *Hearts of Lions*. New York: W. W. Norton & Co., 1988.

Patton, Phil. *Open Road*. New York: Simon & Schuster, 1986.

Plas, van der Rob. *The Bicycle Touring Manual*. San Francisco: Bicycle Books, 1993.

Ritchie, Andrew. *Major Taylor*. San Francisco: Bicycle Books, 1988.

Sloane, Eugene A. *The Complete Book of Bicycling*. New York: Trident Press, 1970.

Smith, Robert A. *A Social History of the Bicycle*. New York: American Heritage Press, 1972.

Stevens, Thomas. *Around the World on a Bicycle*. Abridged ed. Tucson, Ariz.: Seven Palms Press, 1984.

———. *Around the World on a Bicycle*. Vol. 1. New York: Charles Scribner's Sons, 1887.

Willard, Frances E. *How I Learned to Ride the Bicycle*. Sunnyvale, Calif.: Fair Oaks Publishing, 1991.

Winning, Robert. *Bicycling Across America*. Berkeley, Calif.: Wilderness Press, 1988.

"The World Awheel." *Munsey* magazine. May 1896.

ABOUT THE AUTHOR

DAVID LAMB is an eight-time Pulizer Prize nominee who has traveled the world for twenty-five years as a *Los Angeles Times* correspondent. He is the author of four widely praised previous books. He lives in northern Virginia, near the bike path that runs along the Potomac.

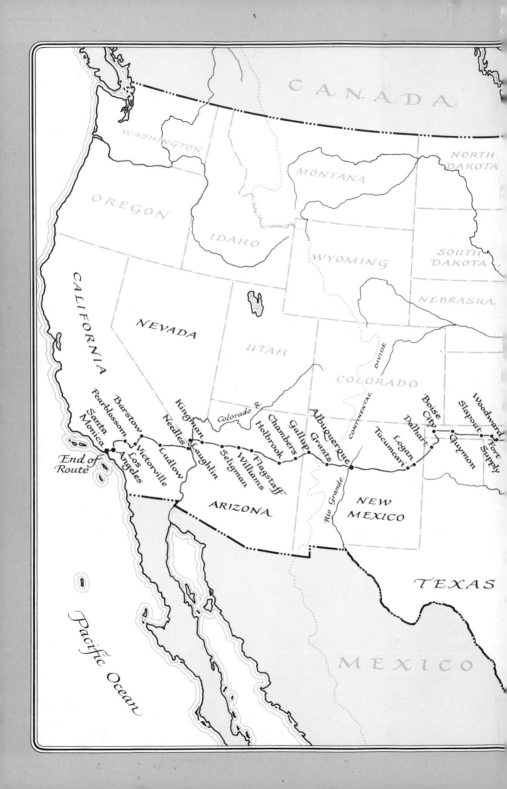